SCOTLAND
END TO END

First published 2012 by Mountain Media Productions Ltd

Mountain Media Productions Ltd
Old Glen Road
Newtonmore
Inverness-shire PH20 1EB

www.mountain-media.co.uk

Text by Cameron McNeish for Mountain Media Productions Ltd

Photography by Richard Else for Mountain Media Productions Ltd

Maps drawn by Gregor McNeish

Design and layout by Gregor McNeish

Set in 11.5pt Aldine Light / Trajan

Printed by Butler Tanner & Dennis, Somerset

ISBN-13: 978-0-9562957-3-6

Contact details, accommodation and travel information are correct at the time
of going to press. Significant changes will be posted on **www.mountain-media.co.uk**

The **Leave No Trace** principles are reproduced by kind permission of the
Leave No Trace Center for Outdoor Ethics, Boulder, CO, USA.

While every effort has been made to contact copyright holders Mountain Media
Production Ltd apologises for any who have been inadvertently overlooked.

The maps in this book are intended as a rough guide and should not be used for
navigational purposes in the field.

SCOTLAND
END TO END

Walking the Gore-Tex®
Scottish National Trail

CAMERON MCNEISH AND RICHARD ELSE

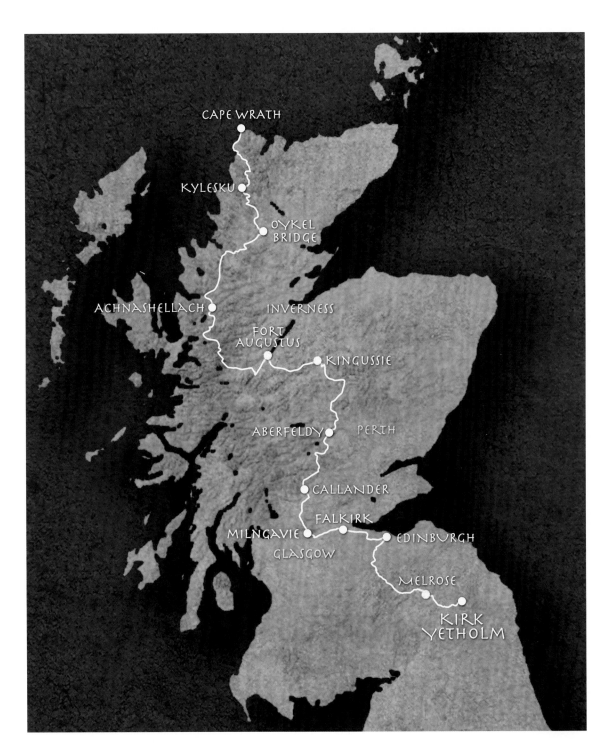

CAPE WRATH

KYLESKU

OYKEL
BRIDGE

ACHNASHELLACH   INVERNESS

FORT
AUGUSTUS
                                    KINGUSSIE

                         PERTH
ABERFELDY

                CALLANDER

                FALKIRK
MILNGAVIE   EDINBURGH
GLASGOW

                              MELROSE

KIRK
YETHOLM

CONTENTS

Cameron camping on the Gore-Tex Scottish National Trail

Acknowledgements

Writing and photographing a book can often feel like a solitary experience especially when the fun part, the walking part, is over and you have to sit down in front of a computer and produce something tangible. That's the hard bit. It's also when you remember everyone who has contributed something to the whole process.

Roger Smith has been a friend and colleague for many years now and his keen editing eye and resolute patience have been a Godsend. The whole world loves a volunteer and Roger generously volunteered to take on that most excruciatingly grinding task – compiling an index. Roger, we love you!

We are both very fortunate in having family members who are infinitely more talented than we are and once again Gregor McNeish has pulled out all the stops to design a beautiful book. James and Liv Else produced the marvellous music for the television shows, music that highlighted the glorious landscapes we walked through.

Despite having been born and raised on a Borders farm and having now moved into the posh Edinburgh suburb of Morningside our film cameraman Dominic Scott condescended to work with us again. But while you can take the man out of the farm you can never take the farm out of the man and we're a little concerned that his new neighbours may not appreciate a few Cheviot yews in the back garden.

Special thanks, as always, goes to our long suffering Editor at Television Sport, BBC Scotland. We suspect David Harron only tholes us because we bring a level of sanity to the totally unpredictable world of recording the ups and downs of Scottish football. Thanks also to our Commissioning Editor at BBC Scotland, Ewan Angus, who has shown real faith in our annual Christmas walking programmes. Who would have believed they would successfully compete with the Wizard of Oz and Chitty Chitty Bang Bang?

Many thanks also to our wives, Gina and Meg, for putting up with the long absences while we were away walking and photographing. Gina has shown great patience when Cameron has dragged her off on the odd wet weekend to check sections of the route, and once again Meg has exhibited her enormous talent as a television producer to keep us on the straight and narrow in all those hotel bars up and down the length of the country.

Finally, our warm appreciation to WL Gore, manufacturers of Gore-Tex® and sponsors of the Gore-Tex® Scottish National Trail, who have shown great faith in another of our projects. Special thanks to Anna McNamara and Willie Fletcher for their unfailing enthusiasm and encouragement and we hope the trail will be something they will be proud of in the years to come.

Cameron McNeish and Richard Else, *Newtonmore, August 2012*

The first view of the Eildon Hills from Dere Street

PROLOGUE

The church bells of Kirk Yetholm were striking nine when I left the Border Hotel, an establishment whose luxuries are more usually appreciated by those who have just completed a long, hard walk rather than those just starting one. Kirk Yetholm is the northern terminus of the 429km/267-mile Pennine Way, the long-distance trail that follows the spine of England from Edale in the Peak District to the Scottish Borders, but I was heading off in the opposite direction. Edinburgh was my destination, the first leg of a long journey that would see me walk the length of Scotland, 756km/470 miles from the Border to Cape Wrath, the most north-westerly point on the Scottish mainland.

The notion of a long-distance trail that runs the length of the country isn't a new one. Mountain gangrel Hamish Brown has long favoured the idea of a long-distance walking route through Scotland and indeed followed his own version of the route while writing his book *Hamish's Groat's End Walk*, a UK-length walk from John o' Groats to Land's End, back in the late 1970s. Another of his books, *From the Pennines to the Highlands*, offers a route between Byrness in Northumberland and Milngavie and the start of the West Highland Way and was very useful in my own route planning through a part of Scotland that I was least familiar with.

Despite the lack of an 'official' route, many long-distance walkers have made the trek north through Scotland. Every year hardy 'end-to-enders' take the long road north from Land's End, working their way over the undulating moors of Cornwall and Devon and on into the Midlands before heading east to pick up the Pennine Way in Edale, Derbyshire, the line of which brings them north to the Scottish Border. From there a variety of routes lead them ultimately to John o'Groats. The LEJOG (Land's End to John o'Groats) is an ambitious walk, there's little doubt about that, one that I'd long considered myself, but a variety of issues have always made me put it on the back burner. The sheer length of time it takes to walk from Land's End to John O'Groats is probably the biggest factor – I'm not sure I want to be away from home for three or four months.

While I've been a long-time advocate of lightweight backpacking, living in the wild places and doing all we can to protect such wonderful areas, I find that two or three weeks backpacking is as much as I need, or want, at a time. I love my home,

I like to be close to my wife and children, and nowadays my grandchildren, and so the time it takes to walk the entire length of Britain has appealed less to me as I've become older. I have too many other interests to spend a quarter of the year participating in just one of them. The problem is that once the notion of travelling from one end of the country to the other becomes lodged in your brain it's hard to shrug it off. It becomes a monkey on your back, a monkey that every so often begins to bounce around and shriek in your ear. I reckoned the only way to dislodge the beast was to do it, but instead of taking three or four months to walk it I took a bike and cycled it in a fortnight.

I guess the LEJOG was a 'bucket-list' thing, something to do before I became too old and infirm to even think about it. The bike gave me an opportunity to complete it in a reasonable time, while still putting in a fair amount of physical effort, and having some fun along the way, but my reasons for walking the length of Scotland were curiously different. The LEJOG cycle trip was a bit of a challenge and we wanted to complete the thousand-mile (1600km) route in a fortnight. I cycled the route with my oldest friend, Hamish Telfer. We met as 14-year-olds when we both joined the West of Scotland Harriers at the same time, so there was a Last of the Summer Wine aspect to the trip. As teenagers and young men we shared many adventures together, in athletics and later on the hills of Scotland, and I suspect there was an element of trying to regain something of our lost youth in going off to cycle the length of the country in our early 60s. I don't think it had anything to do with a middle-aged crisis – we were too old for that. We weren't so much MAMILs (middle-aged men in lycra) as OFILs (old farts in lycra).

Ernest Hemingway once wrote in praise of the bike as a mode of transport. "It is by riding a bicycle that you learn the contours of a country best," he said, "since you have to sweat up the hills and coast down them. Thus you remember them as they actually are, while in a motor car only a high hill impresses you, and you have no such accurate remembrance of country you have driven through as you gain by riding a bicycle." I think he's correct to a certain degree but on the LEJOG bike ride I did notice that each day the countryside tended to flash past us.

The off! Leaving the comfort of The Border Hotel in Kirk Yetholm with cameraman Dominic Scott and producer Margaret Wicks

The bicycle, although a wonderful mode of transport, and the tarmac roads we were obliged to use, tended to sequester us to a large extent from the countryside we were passing through and I knew from long experience that by walking I could become much more intimate with the land, there was a greater opportunity to hear its heartbeat, to walk to its rhythms rather than my own. And that was how I wanted to travel through Scotland.

Early winter snow covers the Pentland Hills to the east of the trail

As I mentioned earlier, my motives for walking the length of Scotland were different from those of wanting to travel the length of the UK. First of all I believed passionately that Scotland should have a long-distance trail that ran the length of the country, and secondly, I wanted to walk through my own country of birth, simply to get to know it better, to weigh up aspects of its character and culture, to remind myself of its history and factions, its nuances and its remarkable diversity of landscape at a time when this small nation was beginning a process of re-discovery and questioning if it could go it alone outside the comfort zone of the UK, if it could survive and prosper as a separate nation and not just a place known as northern Britain. I wanted to ask the same questions, and re-discover the land of my birth for myself, especially those areas that I wasn't so familiar with. Forty years of climbing mountains in the highlands and islands of Scotland had given me a pretty broad knowledge of those areas and I've lived in the Scottish highlands since I was in my twenties. But I wasn't quite so familiar with the rolling hills and dales of that great chunk of land that lies between the Glasgow/Edinburgh line and the border with England. That would be newish territory for me and I was keen to see it and compare it with those areas I was more familiar with, all in the context of a long journey through it.

One thing I was very much aware of was that Scotland has a massive potential for more long-distance trails. Even if there are currently no resources for building new paths, planners should be aware of the potential, and not permit new developments that would act as impediments to creating future trails. In that respect I was keen to travel through some of the wild areas of Scotland before we lose them, or at least lose the wild aspect of them. According to reports from Scottish Natural Heritage we are losing those areas that can be described as wild at an alarming rate, mostly due to the development of renewable energy, onshore wind power in particular. Endless articles and even whole books have been written about the pros and cons of wind as an energy source so I don't intend to repeat them here, but the rapid development of industrial-sized wind developments is having a very negative effect on the wild areas of Scotland, just as large-scale commercial forestry did in the 1940s and 1950s. I was keen, on one hand, to see what cumulative effect these wind farms were having on the scenery of Scotland, and on the other hand, to enjoy as much of wild Scotland as I could while it was still truly wild.

In comparison with England and Wales we can boast relatively few routes, although that situation appears to be changing. There are currently 15 'official' National Trails in England and Wales. We have four in Scotland and here they are known as 'official long-distance footpaths'. In terms of 'unofficial' routes there are over 200 routes, all of them in excess of 50km/30 miles, in England and Wales, while currently in Scotland there appear to be about 25. A traditional reluctance to create 'official' routes is partly to blame for Scotland lagging behind, a reluctance that I tentatively share, despite the fact that I've done my fair share in trying to create trails of this type. Up until comparatively recently the hiking convention in Scotland was that people made up their own routes, that by using our traditional freedom to roam we could simply start at point A and walk to point B by using maps and our own common sense. A large network of rights of way, historically collated by the Scottish Rights of Way Society, nowadays known as Scotways, helped in the planning.

Indeed, I recall as a youngster poring over the excellent little book, *Scottish Hill Tracks*, published by the SRWS, spending many pleasurable hours linking rights of way together, making long routes through some of our wildest landscapes. There was a real joy in that kind of planning, a deep and satisfying sense of exploration that can't be experienced if you simply buy a guidebook and then follow signposts all day long. There was for a long time a deep suspicion of anything that might threaten our cherished freedom to roam, and that included the southern attitude to waymarked trails.

I was as indoctrinated in this way of thinking as anyone, and at a press conference in Glasgow in 1979 I was pretty robust in my views about the creation of Scotland's first long-distance walking route, the West Highland Way. The London-based publishers, Constable, had produced the first guide to the route, and to add some muscle to their presentation the company wheeled in John Hillaby, whose book *Journey Through Britain* had been published a number of years previously. Hillaby was an excellent writer, and a strong walker, but he was completely blind to the fact that the Scots had a very different attitude to long-distance walking routes. He also portrayed an immense ignorance of Scotland's hill traditions, customs and laws, a fact that clearly irritated the representative of the Scottish Mountaineering Club. Sandy Cousins was an inveterate stravaiger and a staunch defender of Scottish hill traditions and he didn't like the idea of a long-distance footpath in Scotland one bit. Once Hillaby had completed his bullish, blustering presentation Sandy stood up and tore the whole concept of long-distance trails, or 'Ways', apart. "We've never had them in Scotland and we don't need them now", he roared in his own inimitable manner. "We have *de facto* rights of access in Scotland and don't need signposted paths to show us where to go, to lead us by the hand. Long-distance trails are an English concept that have no place north of the Border".

Sitting beside me was a tall and rather elegant gentleman, a member of the Countryside Commission for Scotland. When Sandy had completed his verbal attack, this gentleman leaned across to me and said quietly: "I agree with much of what Sandy has said but essentially he's wrong. The West Highland Way is going to become very popular". The gentleman was the eminent writer and mountaineer W.H. Murray and he was prophetic in his assertion.

Cameron in his own back yard – Glen Banchor, linking the Cairngorms and the Monadhliath

Almost 35 years later the West Highland Way has become the most popular trail in the country, with some 85,000 people using the path every year, of whom it's believed over 30,000 walk the entire route between Milngavie and Fort William. Three other official long-distance footpaths exist in Scotland– the Southern Upland Way between Portpatrick in Galloway and Cockburnspath on the Berwickshire coast; the Great Glen Way between Inverness and Fort William; and the Speyside Way between Buckie and Newtonmore. The latter two were set up under the auspices of Scottish Natural Heritage (SNH), though not without immense and almost insurmountable difficulties in negotiating access with various landowners. Even after almost 30 years of negotiations and the advent of the very positive access arrangements under the Land Reform (Scotland) Act of 2003, the final stage of the Speyside Way between Aviemore and Newtonmore is still not complete.

The conical form of Sgur Dubh – North West Sutherland

It's perhaps because of these time-consuming difficulties that SNH appear reluctant to 'create' any more official long-distance paths in Scotland, but the organisation has indicated that it would be happy to support local government initiatives or community groups who want to create their own routes. Despite the current economic difficulties such 'unofficial' routes are not short in number – SNH list 20 of them and some look very appealing and could, with some promotion, take some of the pressure off the West Highland Way which is suffering from over popularity and overuse. All of these routes, known collectively as *Scotland's Great Trails*, are nationally promoted and each one is distinctively waymarked, largely off-road and has a range of visitor services. With each trail being at least 40km/25 miles in length, all are suitable for multi-day journeys as well as day trips.

But there are others too. A guidebook to the East Highland Way, a lovely route between Fort William and Aviemore was recently published, and I've attended meetings of potential stakeholders who would like to tie down an exact route for the Cape Wrath Trail, between Fort William and the country's most north-westerly point, potentially the toughest and most exciting trail of all. A number of potential routes between Fort William and Cape Wrath have been publicised in recent times but there is an argument that suggests it would be in everyone's best interests if the route became officially formalised.

When BBC Scotland asked me to come up with a long walk through the northern county of Sutherland a few years ago I became intrigued by the idea of working out a logical route, linking as many little villages (preferably with a good pub and accommodation) as I could. Since then I've written a book about the Sutherland Trail; another about the Skye Trail, a marvellous route between the northern tip of Trotternish and Broadford; we made a television programme called The Hebridean Trail, a long walk and bike ride through the Outer Hebrides; and made another television programme about a Scottish Coast to Coast walk between Aberdeen and Knoydart. In the course of researching the route I've thoroughly enjoyed the Kirk Yetholm to Edinburgh section, a wonderful walk in its own right; I've walked between Glasgow and Aviemore and between Milngavie and Fort William, visiting the best of the Central Highlands en route; and I've walked between Fort William and Cape Wrath, the notional Cape Wrath Trail, a route that I've previously described as being one of the most challenging and magnificent long-distance walks in Europe.

To link the various routes together has been the challenge of the Gore-Tex Scottish National Trail, a route that I believe can stand comparison with the best walking routes anywhere in the world.

CHAPTER 1

THE BORDER TO EDINBURGH

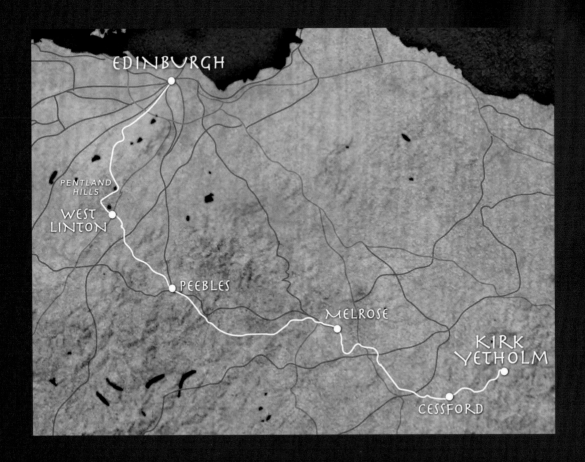

"This is most beautiful! The hedges are now full of shepherds rose, honeysuckles, and all sorts of wild flowers, so that you are upon a grass walk, with this most beautiful of all flower gardens and shrubberies on your one hand, and with the corn on the other...." William Cobbett

Start: Kirk Yetholm.

Finish: Edinburgh (Water of Leith Conservation Trust Visitor Centre, Slateford).

Distance: 130km/80 miles approx.

Additional route information
Official guide to St Cuthbert's Way by Ron Shaw (Mercat Press). Official guide to the Southern Upland Way by Roger Smith (Mercat Press). Tweed Trails leaflets available locally or through www.visitscottishborders.com. Guide to the Water of Leith Walkway available from the Water of Leith Conservation Trust. Websites: www.stcuthbertsway.info, www.southernuplandway.gov.uk, www.waterofleith.org.uk

General information
For more information on accommodation, visitor attractions etc, go to www.visitscottishborders.com and www.visitedinburgh.com. For more information on public transport go to www.travelinescotland.com or phone 0871 200 22 33.

The first good viewpoint on the trail is just south of Town Yetholm from the slopes of Wideopen Hill

Kirk Yetholm to Edinburgh

from the Border to the Capital

While Kirk Yetholm is best known as the northern terminus of the Pennine Way, it is really only one half of the twin communities of Kirk and Town Yetholm. Straddling the Bowmont River, which runs deep into the heart of the Cheviots, Yetholm lies less than two kilometres from the English/Scottish border. Appropriately, the name Yetholm means a 'gateway', a portal to either Scotland or England depending on which way you are travelling. Since I wanted to walk the length of Scotland it was important to begin, not from the village of Kirk Yetholm as such, but from the Scotland/England border itself, a straggling line that runs from just north of Berwick-on-Tweed to the Solway Firth. The borderline lay just to the east of Kirk Yetholm so, the day before I was to begin walking north, I found myself heading in the opposite direction to technically begin the Gore-Tex Scottish National Trail.

The border with England runs for 154 km/96 miles between the River Tweed on the east coast and the Solway Firth in the west. It represents Scotland's only land border and it has rarely been a peaceful place. Like the Anglo/Welsh border there has been a long history of raiding and plundering, battling and mixed allegiances. Border families frequently changed sides, swearing allegiance to whoever was in their best interests at the time. Indeed, the Borderers tended to show loyalty to their family rather than their nation, the result of often just not knowing whether they were Scots or English!

Families living in areas like Liddesdale, Redesdale and Tynedale, through which the regular trade routes between north and south ran, were often plundered and harassed by marauding armies who would demand hospitality and provisioning as they passed through. If they didn't get it, the soldiers simply burnt all before them, destroying crops and stealing livestock. It's no wonder the Borders people themselves turned to lawlessness, known as 'border reiving', and the areas immediately on both sides of the border became known as the Debatable Lands.

Between the 13th and 17th centuries, reiving became a way of life for many Borderers. For the ordinary people, it was the only way to survive the changing political fortunes of the larger, more influential families of the region. Raiding of sheep and cattle took place and not always across the border. Reiving also happened between opposing families in both England and Scotland. These were people who were displaced, often abandoned, and their allegiance was not to a Scots or an English crown, but to their own family, or clan. Some of these inter-family feuds would last for generations, usually set off by some obscure, real or imagined argument. In time these Border reivers became recognised as great soldiers, largely because of their excellent horsemanship. They were recruited for both Scots and English armies but records show that they were rarely reliable. Indeed, at battles such as Ancrum Moor in 1545, Borderers changed sides in mid-battle to curry favour with the likely victors, and at the Battle of Pinkie Cleugh in 1547 it is said that the Scottish and English Borderers blethered to each other in the midst of battle, and on being spotted put on a show of fighting. This might suggest the soldiers considered themselves to be Borderers first and foremost, Scots or English second, a notion that is not uncommon in the Borders even today.

I followed the Pennine Way out of the village, passing a house with its garden symbolically decorated with old walking boots. Instead of flowers and plants it looked as though this particular garden was growing boots. Lots of them, old boots, gnarled boots, moss-covered boots and even some newish-looking boots. Jackie Wilks runs the Laughing Donkeys hostel in Kirk Yetholm – she used to keep a couple of donkeys in her garage across the road, but now she collects boots from walkers who have completed the Pennine Way. "Walkers tend to develop a very close and almost loving relationship with their boots, especially if those boots

Proof that the Pennine Way is a slog! Discarded boots form an ornamental garden in Kirk Yetholm

have carried them successfully for 270 miles on the Pennine Way," she told me. "Rather than throw their boots away a lot of walkers hand them in here where I put them in the garden, put some flowers in them and look after them in their retirement. It's like an old folks' home for retired boots." I loved the notion of that and promised Jackie I would send her my own boots once I'd completed my walk at Cape Wrath. Originally from Hertfordshire, Jackie moved to Livingston in West Lothian in 1989 and then ten years ago she settled in Kirk Yetholm. She told me she came to the village because she bought a horse, then a couple of donkeys and now she's fallen in love with the area. She's never walked the Pennine Way herself and reckons she wouldn't be capable of doing it now, but she often takes her dogs for long walks on the last stretch of the route at nearby Halterburn.

The road climbed over the brow of a hill then dropped down into the Halterburn Valley where a grassy path lifted me high above the green pastures and wooded slopes and across the south face of a hill called Green Humbleton. Unusually, the landscapes to the north were a patchwork of low-lying fields but to the south, in England, the hills rose in a complex array of rounded ridges and bald tops – the foothills of The Cheviot, the pride of Northumberland and one of the loneliest regions in England. Indeed old Alfred Wainwright, the Patron Saint of English fell-walking, when writing about the area in his *Pennine Way Companion*, described the traverse of the Cheviot hills from Byrness to Kirk Yetholm as "the longest and loneliest of all".

The grassy track continued to a hill called Stob Rig, passing the ancient Stob Stones. These are known locally as the 'Gypsy Stobs' and the name relates to the tradition that the stones mark the spot where Kirk Yetholm's gypsy kings and queens were crowned. Kirk Yetholm was often used as a refuge for groups and individuals fleeing from one country to the other, particularly gypsies. One story suggests that during a battle in France in the 17th century, a soldier with Romany origins rescued a British officer. The officer, a Captain Bennet, apparently held land in the Yetholm area and in gratitude to the soldier who had saved his life he made this, plus some cottages, available to the soldier and his descendants. In the late 19th century Scotland's last gypsy King and Queen, Charles and Esther Faa Blythe, were crowned here at Kirk Yetholm. Six donkeys drew the coronation carriage, and you can still see the little house, called the Gypsy Palace, where the King and Queen lived.

It's been suggested the Stob Stones could also be boundary stones, set up to mark the line of the Border. Although the present Border is a little to the east, this point was regarded as fixed as far back as 1222, although the first reference to this border was apparently made in 1173 when the River Tweed marked the frontier.

In 1237, the border was legally established by the Treaty of York between England and Scotland, with the exception of a small area around Berwick, which was taken by England in 1482. Today, an old wall and fence marks the present national border, the man-made line that separates two nations, two cultures and two parliaments. Following the 1707 Treaty of Union, which united Scotland and England to form the Kingdom of Great Britain, the Border continued to form the boundary of two distinct legal jurisdictions as the treaty between the two countries guaranteed the continued separation of English and Scots law.

Curiously, I felt little emotion standing there beside the fence that separates Scotland and England. Perhaps we've become so accustomed to being British that political boundaries like this become a little meaningless – for the moment at least. With a Scottish National Party Government ruling successfully in Scotland, and a Tory-led coalition Government in Westminster, there is every chance the people of Scotland will shortly vote for independence. The Tories have never been popular in Scotland and the Tory/Liberal Democrat coalition has few friends north of the Border. Time could be right for the Scottish Nationalists and their charismatic, and extremely able leader Alex Salmond. Indeed, when Edinburgh Zoo was recently gifted two pandas from China, Mr Salmond made the remark that Scotland now had more pandas than Tory MPs, a comment that highlights Scotland's traditional contempt for the Conservative and Unionist Party!

It was partly because of the political atmosphere in Scotland that I grew interested in walking the length of the country. Was Scotland comfortable enough in its own abilities and potential to leave the not-always-cosy embrace of the Union and go it alone in the world? Did the Scots, a nation of people who in the past had only been too willing to be subservient, feel their time had arrived? And could Scotland, minus its traditional industries like steelmaking, mining and shipbuilding, survive on tourism and the nascent industry of renewable energy? In the context of my long walk I hoped to get a feel for the answers to some of these questions, but above all I wanted to experience the diversity of landscapes and horizons that Scotland had to offer, I wanted to soak myself in the wild lands and the rugged beauty, I wanted to walk the byways of the land, to seek out the quieter places and familiarise myself with an aspect of the nation that rarely makes it into political manifestos. And I could only do that by walking…

As I stood by that old fence I was aware that while technically, this was the beginning of my long walk north, it was just another fence on another hillside. I suspected I might feel differently in the morning when I left Kirk Yetholm to start the walk proper, those mixed emotions that tend to flood through me every time I begin a long walk. But since I had taken the trouble to climb up here to the Anglo/Scots border I was keen to make a decent walk of it. I followed the fence line over White Law, at 436m/1407 feet the highest point of the route, down to a wet and boggy, sheep-infested col before climbing the long and gradual slopes of Steer Rig to the summit of Black Hag with open views over the Cheviots towards the Northumberland coast; in the other direction, only the triple-topped Eildon hills rose from the Border flatlands. The Cheviot itself, 815m/2676ft, was topped by a blanket of grey cloud. In 1878 a traveller and writer, William Weaver Tomlinson, wrote in his *Comprehensive Guide to Northumberland*: "the summit is a desolate looking tract of treacherous moss-hags and oozy peat-flats, traversed by deep sykes and interspersed with black stagnant pools." The mountain doesn't appear to have changed very much.

Gypsy history is integrally linked to Kirk Yetholm. This is the former Gypsy Palace at the end of the Pennine Way

Where the Pennine Way ends, the Gore-Tex Scottish National Trail begins – The Border Hotel at Kirk Yetholm

Below Black Hag another grassy track runs downhill to Old Halterburnhead. This is the official 'alternative' route of the Pennine Way, a lower-level option for those northbound hikers who simply want to get the route over and done with. I stopped for a while by the ruins of the old farmhouse and soaked up the spirit-of-place atmosphere before meeting a couple of Pennine Way walkers who were scurrying down the hill, eager to complete their journey along the spine of England. As we walked back downhill towards Kirk Yetholm it was clear they didn't envy me in the slightest. They had "drunk their fill" of long-distance walking for the moment, and while they didn't dismiss the idea that they might try another long-distance trail in the future, right now they were just delighted to finish. I left them trying to sort out travel arrangements to take them back home to Buckinghamshire, while I checked into the Border Hotel, ordered a coffee and a fruit scone and sat down with my maps, my guidebooks and my dreams.

Kirk Yetholm to Melrose

Distance:	50km/31 miles.
Maps:	This section is covered (in walking order) by Ordnance Survey 1:50,000 Landranger sheets 74 and 73.
Public transport:	Bus service from Kelso to Kirk Yetholm. Buses to Kelso from both Edinburgh and Berwick-on-Tweed rail stations. Buses to Melrose from Edinburgh.
Accommodation:	Hotel, B&Bs and hostel in Kirk Yetholm. Hotels or B&Bs in Morebattle, Jedburgh (3km off route), St Boswells, Newtown St Boswells and Melrose. Youth hostel in Melrose.
Route:	Follow Pennine Way signs out of Kirk Yetholm into the Halterburn Valley and up past Green Humbleton to reach the Border ridge at GR854269. Continue along the ridge to Black Hag (GR863237). Follow Pennine Way alternative route signs down past Old Halterburnhead and back to Kirk Yetholm. From Kirk Yetholm follow St Cuthbert's Way signs through Morebattle, Cessford, Jedfoot, Harestanes, Maxton, Newtown St Boswells, St Boswells and Bowden to Melrose.

Kirk Yetholm is also on the route of St Cuthbert's Way, a 100km/62-mile walk that follows in the footsteps of Cuthbert, a 7th century priest who became Prior of the Celtic monastery at Melrose. The route runs from Melrose Abbey to Lindisfarne in Northumberland and since I was heading for Melrose it seemed a little churlish not to follow in the footsteps of the saint! On a more prosaic note I felt some relief at being able to follow a signposted route for the first couple of days of my route.

Normally my backpacking trips are in the highlands where you can virtually walk where you please and camp where you please. Here in the south I knew that I'd be walking on agricultural land, around fields, on country lanes and along minor roads. I was also a little unsure about wild camping in such an agricultural environment and I was concerned about finding water to drink that wasn't spoiled by sheep or agricultural run-off. Although the Land Reform (Scotland) Act suggests you can camp wild for one or more nights, it does say you should be out of sight of houses and roads. That might not be easy in such landscapes as these, although I also had the option of finding a small inn or bed and breakfast to stay at. Camping isn't the only form of accommodation on a route like this, and while it's probably the most convenient I was looking forward to treating myself occasionally to a bar meal and a hotel bed.

I thought I should treat myself on my first night. If I didn't no-one else would, although it has to be said the staff in the Border Hotel in Kirk Yetholm looked after me very well. Built in 1750 as a coaching inn with a thatched roof, the Border Hotel was originally known as the 'Grey Horse' but in 1893 the thatched roof on the main building was replaced and the name was changed to the 'Border Inn'. In 1898 the gable was built and the name changed again to the 'Border Hotel'. It was here that curmudgeonly old Alfred Wainwright betrayed his reputation as a grumpy meanie. Sprawled in the bar after his own adventures on the Pennine Way, he decided to set up a long-standing tab for everyone who completes the full distance from Edale to Kirk Yetholm. Everyone reaching the Border Hotel would be given a pint of beer on request, and he would pay the bill. Some years later, following the spectacular popularity of the Pennine Way – and the free pint at the end – he changed it to a half pint. That'll teach him to be so generous, so out of character! I was thankful there wasn't a bar at Cape Wrath – I would hate walkers to expect the same generosity from me…

Well fed after a full Scottish breakfast I wandered out from Kirk Yetholm, past the Youth Hostel (it hadn't opened for the summer season yet and has since closed down permanently) and along the riverside path to the bridge over the Bowmont Water that separates Kirk Yetholm from its twin, Town Yetholm. In the 7th

Cameron with the guardian of the old boots, Jackie Wilks

century Yetholm was part of the Kingdom of Northumbria when King Oswy (612-670) granted most of the Bowmont Valley to the monastery at Lindisfarne. There's plenty of evidence of a population even before then, with numerous hill forts, field boundaries and hut platforms almost littering the landscape. In 1304 King Edward I convened a huge gathering in Yetholm to receive the submission of many 'rebellious' Scottish noblemen. After that, relations between England and Scotland became a little hostile and, sadly, Yetholm suffered from its exposed position on the border. In the 1520s and then again in the 1540s it was burned to the ground during Henry VIII's vicious attacks against Scotland.

Other than a gentle stroll along its main street the night before, I didn't see much of Town Yetholm. A pleasant footpath followed the banks of the Bowmont Water so rather than go through the village I followed it, and the St Cuthbert's Way signs, past Duncanhaugh and onto the B6401 below the grassy slopes of Yetholm Law. At the first road junction the signs indicated I should follow the road to Cocklawfoot, where I'd enjoyed some great hillwalking in the past. Past the farm at Clifton I turned off onto an old farm track that climbed gently to an obvious ridge. A drystone wall followed the ridge all the way to the summit of Wideopen Hill, an appropriately named top with a well spread panorama of the surrounding countryside. Here, 368 m/1186ft above sea level, I took the opportunity to sit down, lean against the wall and enjoy the extensive views across to the Cheviots, the lovely rounded hills of the English Border.

Although I was anxious to get some miles under my boots, it was great to sit here for a while and listen to the sound of skylarks, my first of the year. What songsters these little birds are, flying higher and higher and then pouring out a tirade of such warbling intensity as they float back down again. The optimism in their lovely, shrill, melodious singing defies description, an outpouring of such intensely penetrating and passionate joy that it's infectious. In fact it was so infectious I almost skipped down the ridge, over the curiously named Grubbit Law and down to the footbridge over the Kale Water where oystercatchers were dutifully patrolling their patch, screeching in annoyance at my disturbance. The woods were full of spring birdsong, which compensated for the wee bit of tarmac bashing that lay before me. Climbing up the road into the village was hot work but I craved caffeine. I had plenty of water to drink but mid-morning is coffee time, if you can get hold of the stuff. There was a hotel in Morebattle but there didn't appear to be anyone around – maybe it was too early in the day. I thought there might be a tea-room or coffee shop but there wasn't. Ironically, as if to frustrate me further, I came across a sign pointing to Teapot Street, but there was no teapot, or tearoom, to be seen anywhere.

There was nothing else for it. I found a quiet corner behind a wall and got out the stove. No point in being self-sufficient if you can't brew yourself a coffee when you feel like it. As the water warmed I looked through a leaflet I had found. It might not have had a coffee or tea-room, but Morebattle once had its own poet. Robert Davidson (1778-1855) had apparently been largely forgotten until a plaque was erected to his memory at the churchyard gate in 2008. A volume of his poems, *Leaves from a Peasant's Cottage Drawer*, was republished in a new edition and it would appear that Davidson was another example of a Borders peasant poet, in the line of Robert Burns, or James Hogg, the Ettrick Shepherd. As something of a Burns and Hogg fan I promised myself I would check Robert Davidson's work when I got home. We can't have too many ploughman-poets!

Duly refreshed by the caffeine fix I tramped along the B6401 road out of Morebattle, studiously avoiding the grassy verges that were deeply rutted from the tyres of agricultural vehicles. Just past the delicately named Cowbog Farm I turned off the main road and followed a minor road across some fields towards the gaunt remains of the 15th century Cessford Castle and then down to the two rows of terraced houses that make up Cessford village. It's clear from its stocky shape and thick walls that Cessford Castle was built as a stockade, created for the dual purposes of defence and protection. There is little that is fanciful or boastful or even comfortable in its plain, solid architecture – this fortification was obviously intended to withstand regular assault, and for a long time, during the turbulent years between the 14th and 16th centuries when the Kers held the honorary title of Warden of the Middle Marches, it did just that.

The castle was put under siege in 1523 by the Earl of Surrey (the man who had defeated the Scots at the Battle of Flodden) when Cessford successfully held out against English artillery, and was again attacked by the English in 1545 during one of Henry VIII's campaigns. But the English weren't the only enemy. The years of the 16th century saw the Kers of Cessford at loggerheads with the Scotts of Buccleuch, their mutual animosity coming to a head when the Kers burned down Catslack Tower near Selkirk in 1548. Among those killed was Elizabeth Scott, Buccleuch's widow, who had been born a Ker of Cessford. In 1607 Sir Robert Ker, later the 1st Earl of Roxburghe, abandoned Cessford Castle for more comfortable accommodation near Melrose. His great-great-grandson, the 5th Earl, eventually moved the family to what is now the very grand Floors Castle near Kelso, a very different fortification from the gaunt Cessford Castle.

Standing in splendid isolation, Cessford Castle was originally built in the mid 15th century by Andrew Ker, an ancestor of the Dukes of Roxburghe

A dirt track made its way between the two terraces towards Cessford Moor and I followed it with some relief. I was now walking on softer tracks, and not the hard tarmac that gives me sore feet, and from the top of the hill I began to follow a series of field verges, with some very pleasant walking along the edges of woods that I felt was spoiled to some extent by vast, prairie-like fields. The majority of my walking and hiking is enjoyed in the open spaces of the Scottish highlands and in this southern section of the Scottish National Trail I was looking forward to rambling through the rural pleasures of a patchworked, green landscape, but where had all the wooded copses gone, the hedgerows and the bush-filled ditches? In 1822, in his book *Rural Rides*, William Cobbett made the following observation:

The custom is in this part of Hertfordshire to leave a border round the ploughed part of the fields to bear grass and make hay from, so that, the grass being now made into hay, every corn field has a close mowed grass walk about 10 feet wide all round it, between the corn and the hedge. This is most beautiful! The hedges are now full of shepherds rose, honeysuckles, and all sorts of wild flowers, so that you are upon a grass walk, with this most beautiful of all flower gardens and shrubberies on your one hand, and with the corn on the other. And thus you go from field to field, the sort of corn, the sort of underwood and timber, the shape and size of the fields, the height of the hedgerows, the height of the trees, all continually varying. Talk of pleasure-grounds indeed!

It doesn't seem so long ago that hedgerows were a fundamental part of the heritage of the British countryside, defining the nature of the landscape and providing a major shelter and food source for a huge variety of mammals, birds and insects. Hedgerows create a vibrant ecosystem, an important nature reserve in our small and (over) intensively farmed country. Sadly they appear to have been sacrificed for the better financial returns of modern intensive farming. According to the Hedgerow Trust, hedges are complex ecosystems and are essential habitats for a wide range of flora and fauna; 21 out of 28 lowland mammal, 69 out of 91 bird and 23 out of 54 butterfly species breed in hedges. In countryside with little or no woodland they are essential for the survival of many bird species. They provide valuable sheltered routes along which wildlife can move more freely across the country between fragmented woodlands, function as screens against bad weather, provide cover for game, contain and shelter stock and crops, act as windbreaks and help control soil erosion.

Of course our countryside can't remain static, but the rate of disappearance of our hedgerows in recent times has been astonishing, an act of vandalism some would suggest since most have been deliberately removed or allowed to fall into dereliction. As recently as 1945 we had over 500,000 miles of hedgerows in the UK but modern intensive farming methods are obviously not compatible with a pretty countryside and flourishing wildlife. Hedgerows were seen as a hindrance to new and mechanised farming methods and our politicians were only too eager to help their demise. Until the mid 1980s, government grants were available to farmers for the removal of hedges for agricultural 'improvement'. Between 1945 and 1993 around half of the hedges in Britain were destroyed. Today, in that topsy-turvy way that politicians think, often because one side shouts louder than the other, government grants are available for the opposite in an enlightened attempt to repair some of the damage. It appears to me that a sustained campaign is now required if the damage done to one of our national treasures is to be redressed.

I crossed Cessford Moor, passed Blakeman's Crag, a rounded eminence that rose from the flatness of the prairie fields, and took a zig-zagging line linking up field verges, footpaths, minor roads and woodland paths until I reached the arrow-straight line of the Roman Road called Dere Street. This ancient route ran from York to the Forth estuary where it met the eastern end of the Antonine Wall, once the northernmost boundary of the Roman Empire. Dere Street was a major supply route to the Roman forts along the eastern section of both Hadrian's Wall and the Antonine Wall. At this point on Dere Street I had reached a junction of the St Cuthbert's Way and the Borders Abbeys Way, a 110km/68-mile route which links the four great ruined abbeys of Kelso, Jedburgh, Melrose and Dryburgh. I'd be visiting Melrose Abbey soon enough but for the moment my route took me downhill, over the Jedfoot Bridge and then across the A698 and onto the fertile banks of the River Teviot.

In the park-like ambience of the riverbank I stopped for a rest, admiring the skills of a horseman who was galloping his mare along the edge of the woods. Spotting me, he trotted his horse over to where I was lying against the concrete block of a suspension bridge. "Where are you going?" he shouted down at me. My hackles rose involuntarily, expecting some monologue about private property and trespass. By this time the horseman had dismounted and I noticed he was smiling. "Sorry, that sounded a bit harsh", he said. "What I meant was are you on a long walk, or just out for the day?" Somewhat relieved, although I had my own well prepared monologue about the access provisions of Scotland's Land Reform Act at the tip of my tongue, I stumbled out the words "Cape Wrath". That shook him!

We chatted for a good ten minutes. He was a local lad, out from nearby Jedburgh to exercise the horse and had done a fair bit of backpacking – the Tour of Mont

Maid Lilliard's monument by the side of Dere Street north of Jedburgh

Blanc, the GR20 in Corsica and the West Highland Way. He rather liked the notion of riding his horse from Kirk Yetholm to Cape Wrath, although he did contend that such a trek would be considerably harder on the horse than on himself. We shook hands and parted – he was heading back to Jedburgh and I was heading north again, this time over a rather impressive suspension bridge into the lovely ornamented grounds of Monteviot House. Floods had washed the original bridge over the River Teviot away in 1997 and the army replaced it with this one, built in 1999. Concrete pillars support it and it has a wooden deck suspended by metal chains with ramped access on both sides to make it suitable for wheelchair users.

Across the river, I was in the grounds of Monteviot House. This is the seat of the Earls of Ancrum and earlier Earls of Lothian and dates from 1740. The gardens were designed in the 1960s by Percy Cane and are well worth a visit. The weather, which had been fine for much of the day, had dulled considerably with a pallid hint of grey over everything, but now the early evening sun had broken through the cloud and cast a shine on everything. The daffodils were in full bloom, and patches of snowdrops and bluebells still looked vibrant and fresh.

Before I tackled the long straight track of Dere Street I dropped off the route for a bit to meet up with a local historian called Walter Elliot (a diversion to the right leads to the Harestanes Countryside Visitor Centre, with displays, shop, toilets and a tea room). Walter has been involved in the archaeology and history of his native Borders for over 50 years. Born in nearby Selkirk and brought up in the remote Ettrick Valley, Walter ran a sawmill and worked as a fencing contractor. He describes himself as a "poor but honest woodcutter" and this work took him to all parts of the Borders where he developed a first-hand familiarity with traces of the past and a curiosity about the various antiquities he picked up along the way. This led him to contact the Mason brothers, great fieldworkers of the Borders, and sparked a passion for fieldworking, particularly at the Roman fort of Newstead.

Walter joked with me that he's the only retired fencing contractor in Selkirkshire who understands Latin. Perhaps his best-known works are the award winning *The Trimontium Story* and his more weighty publications, *The New Minstrelsy of the Scottish Borders 1805-2005* and the recent *Selkirkshire and the Borders*. Walter has not always been in agreement with the archaeological profession but says he was delighted to accept an invitation to receive the Dorothy Marshall Medal Laudation, an award given to an individual who, in a voluntary capacity, has made an outstanding contribution to Scottish archaeological or related work.

"It was very nice to receive this award", he told me, "It's not that I haven't seen eye to eye with some of those in the archaeology field but if you have been a professor of archaeology for 40 years and based your career on one or two finds and then some old retired woodcutter and fencer comes along and says you're wrong, well you won't be best pleased. If something was stated as being correct in 1840 then it would never be challenged. However, these days folk are more prepared to debate things."

I was keen to learn from Walter the story of the Battle of Ancrum Moor because I would shortly be passing by the site of the 16th century skirmish, but before that I had to find somewhere to camp for the night. Leaving Walter at Harestanes I returned to the Monteviot Estate and followed St Cuthbert's Way signs through the estate. It had been a long day and I was beginning to feel a bit weary. The thought of lying down and cooking some supper suddenly had great appeal. It was time to look for somewhere to camp, and that meant looking for fresh water. The path emerged from the Monteviot woods at an unclassified road and continued in its straight Roman road designer way between twin hedgerows. Patches of woodland dotted the landscape and now and then the view opened up enough to reveal the line of Dere Street stretching ahead of me. Originally known as Agricola's Road, it didn't stretch the imagination too much to think that St Cuthbert used it himself.

Dere Street follows a long, low ridge, with huge prairie fields on one side and on the other, just beyond some sheep pastures, the busy A68 road. By a touch of good fortune I noticed the sinking sun glint on some very small puddles in a field and when I investigated I realised it was a spring, a small seep that quickly evolved into a tiny stream. There was a patch of flat ground close by, beside a drystone wall, a good spot to spend the night, my first camp on the Scottish National Trail. Settling down to the sounds of the countryside was nothing short of idyllic. A dog fox barked not far away, perhaps a little unsettled at my presence. Owls called back and forth from the nearby woods and oystercatchers and peewits kept their calls going until dark. At one point I heard some rustling beside me and when I looked out I disturbed a roe deer that suddenly took off in fright, around a tree and over the wall behind me. Its beautiful, graceful movement as it arched over the wall took my breath away.

Things were different in the morning. It had rained heavily in the small hours and I woke to a damp and misty dawn with rain still splattering on the tent. It's sometimes difficult to get moving under such conditions so I brewed some tea and made porridge from the warm comfort of my sleeping bag. Nature's call, probably the effect of the tea, eventually forced me out of the sleeping bag and the tent.

The westernmost of the Eildon Hills seen from the small lochan that is popular with local fishermen

As usual, once on the move things didn't feel so bad and I enjoyed the easy walking along Dere Street. A short distance along the trail a prominent ridge, Lilliard's Edge, lies about 2km from Ancrum and its south-east slopes were the site of the Battle of Ancrum Moor. The evening before, Walter Elliot had explained to me that the battle took place in 1545 during the War of the Rough Wooing, a curious name that covered a very volatile period in Scotland's history.

Not long before his reign drew to an end, Henry VIII was very keen to secure an alliance with Scotland by betrothing his son Edward (by wife number three, Jane Seymour) to the one-year-old Mary, Queen of Scots. When his proposals were rejected by the Scottish Parliament (the situation was complicated by religious differences in Scotland, some Protestants being more sympathetic to the Protestant English crown, while Catholic support was clearly for alliance with France) he pursued the matter by launching a ruthless war against the Scots – the so-called 'Rough Wooing'. Henry's Warden of the Marches, the Earl of Hertford, marched north with his army and laid waste to much of southern Scotland, reaching Edinburgh in May 1544.

The following year the pillaging and destruction of the Borders continued, this time under the direction of Sir Ralph Evers, Warden of the Middle Marches. He had promised Henry that he would take the whole of southern Scotland south of the Forth and Clyde. The King responded by promising him all the territory he could conquer in the Merse, Teviotdale and Lauderdale. Inspired by the King's promise, Evers, along with Sir Ralph Layton, burned down the town of Melrose, destroying Melrose Abbey in the process. The Abbey was the ancestral burial place of the Douglas family and the tombs of their ancestors were opened and desecrated, the exposed human remains scattered to the winds. The pair also burned down Broomhouse Tower, where the lady of the house, her children and servants all perished. These atrocities brought together two erstwhile rivals, the Earl of Arran, regent for the infant Mary, and the Earl of Angus, head of the house of Douglas. These two had once been bitter foes but Angus' estates had been brutally razed by Hertford and some of his lands given over to Evers. He promised to join the Earl of Arran and would witness Evers' title deeds "on their backs with sharp pens and red ink".

On 12th February 1545, the 5,000-strong English army was encamped on Ancrum Moor when a small army under the cautious command of the Earl of Angus approached them. The English were well aware that the Scots force was tiny in comparison with their vastly superior force of Borderers and German and Spanish mercenaries. The Angus army amounted to a mere 1,200 men but they were expecting the arrival of more reinforcements from George Leslie, the Earl of

Rothes and Scott of Buccleuch. Cautiously, Angus approached the English force and deployed his small army ready for battle but out of sight of his enemy. Some riders dismounted and led away their horses to the rear but the English mistakenly thought the Scots were retreating and moved forward to the brow of the ridge only to discover the Scots army waiting for them. With the dazzling light of the setting sun in their eyes, the English attack floundered and mayhem broke out. The English eventually lost 800 men and Evers and Layton were killed. Even more soldiers were taken prisoner and it's said that many of the English Borderers, in the heat of battle, decided to change sides. It was apparently ever thus!

One amusing story from the Battle of Ancrum Moor claims that the Lady Lilliard, in an attempt to avenge the death of her lover who was killed by the English, fought in the battle but was injured several times. She finally died from her wounds and a stone on the site of the battlefield is known as the Lilliard Stone in remembrance of her. The following piece of doggerel engraved on a plaque on the 19th century monument suggests her story may well have been the result of someone's over-fertile imagination:

Fair maiden Lilliard
lies under this stane
little was her stature
but muckle was her fame
upon the English loons
she laid monie thumps
and when her legs were cuttit off
she fought upon her stumps.

I left the site of the battle, and Lilliard's monument, with a smile on my face, the thought of a maiden laying about the English soldiers on two bloody stumps being just a touch of exaggeration too far! But why let the truth spoil a good story?

The sun sets on Dere Street. Although not far from the busy A68, this former Roman Road is quiet and undisturbed

Was I not in the Scottish Borders where tales and legends abound? The story of the maiden Lilliard is as good as any of them.

A final stretch of the heavily overgrown Dere Street took me towards a minor road that led to the village of Maxton on the River Tweed, the birthplace of the medieval scholar, John Duns Scotus. Duns (Scotus was merely a nickname that identified him as a Scot) was a Franciscan priest who was believed to be one of the most important philosopher-theologians of the Middle Ages. His specialities were certainly not lightweight – the semantics of religious language; the problem of universals; divine illumination and the nature of human freedom. Enjoying my own human freedom now that the rain had gone off, I followed St Cuthbert's Way along riverside paths that took me to the edge of St Boswells and then into neighbouring Newtown St Boswells, where I enjoyed a soup and sandwich lunch in an excellent café-cum-bookshop, the Mainstreet Trading Company. An elderly couple, sitting at a table next to me, saw my pack at the front door and asked where I was heading for.

I'm not sure they believed me when I replied, "Cape Wrath, all going well".

A minor road soon turned into another footpath alongside the Bowden Burn, which I crossed by a footbridge near a grand house that goes by the curious name of Maxpoffle, apparently of Norman/French origin. On the north side of the burn stands the village of Bowden, with some firm connections to St Cuthbert and St Aidan. The name is thought to derive from St Boisel, the preceptor of Cuthbert. An area close by was once known as Lessudden, which may originally have been called Lis-Aidan, or the residence of Aidan. By the time I reached the village the rain had returned so I didn't hang around. A path led from the village over what looked like an area of parkland before turning sharp right in a wooded area and then northwards up to the high col that separates the two most northerly of the three Eildons, an area I knew well and a familiar Borders landmark. The three conical mounds of the Eildons are the remains of a volcanic lava flow that, millions of years ago, intruded into the underground sandstone. Eons of weathering by wind, rain and ice have since exposed the mass into the three distinct lumps we know today, the Trimontium of the Romans. If this kind of prosaic geological description leaves you a little cold, then consider this. Legend claims the Eildons were formed not by volcanic activity but by the supernatural powers of Michael Scot the Wizard, who was ordered by the Devil to split a single Eildon mountain into three separate hills.

I have to confess that I find the name of this so-called wizard a bit disappointing. Surely wizards should be called something a little grander, something more otherworldly like Merlin, or Gandalf or even Lord Voldemort? Michael Scot sounds more like the village bookie, or an accountant, or even worse, a banker! Despite his name Michael Scot became a legend but there is little doubt that he did exist. According to many written accounts he was a 13th century philosopher who had studied at Oxford, Paris and Toledo universities and because of his subject became known as Michael Mathematicus. It's believed he was the court astrologer and physician to Frederick the Second, the Holy Roman Emperor known as Frederick the Great. Sir Walter Scott mentioned him in his *Lay of the Last Minstrel* and James Hogg, the Ettrick Shepherd, wrote about him in his book, *The Three Perils of Man*. The Scottish novelist John Buchan also referred to him in his 1924 book *The Three Hostages*.

But Michael Scot the Wizard may have another claim to fame, something infinitely more important than philosophy, mathematics or turning a single Eildon mountain into three. It has been suggested that he is the father of Scots whisky! Surviving copies of manuscripts attributed to Scot refer to the distillation of *aqua vitae* (water of life), sometimes known as *aqua ardens* (meaning burning water), the earliest name for distilled alcohol. In the Middle Ages people distilled spirits and used them to cure their ills, much as we do today I guess, but I really like the reference to whisky by James Hogg. The Ettrick Shepherd wrote, "If a body can just find oot the exac' proper proportion and quantity that ought to be drunk every day and keep to that, I verily throw that he might leeve forever without dying at all, and that doctors and kirkyards would go oot o' fashion". I'll certainly drink to that.

Some time later Thomas the Rhymer, a 13th century bard and seer, claims to have been spirited away by the queen of the fairies, and spent seven years in Elfland, which was apparently deep below the Eildon Hills! Others say Merlin, the great wizard at the court of King Arthur, was stoned to death and buried at nearby Drumelzier, on the banks of the Tweed. Less fanciful, but still fascinating, is the fact that the Eildon's North Hill was once the site of a sizeable ancient settlement, the home of the ancient Selgovae tribe. Archaeologists suggest there could have been as many as 300 hut circles here about 2,000 years ago. Later, the Romans used the site as a fort and signal station.

I wandered down the hill into Melrose, the blood-red mud of the hillside caking my boots and lower legs. Just before I left the path for the tarmac of the town I found a little stream where I tried to wash as much of the clinging mud off as possible. I knew there was a campsite in Melrose but it tended to fill up with caravans and motor campers and since the rain was now streaming down I reckoned I should treat myself to a night in a hotel. The thought of a warm room and a bar meal was enough to overcome my normal love of camping. Walking into town I convinced myself that it's wild camping that I enjoy, not campsite camping, so plumped for the first hotel I found. Next morning, after a very comfortable night in the excellent Burts Hotel, I had to face some wet and windy weather and a long day of walking. The well-signposted route of St Cuthbert's Way finished at

Melrose Abbey and now I'd be following the Southern Upland Way through Galashiels, over the hill to Yair and then up through the forest to the high point of the route south of Edinburgh, the Minch Moor. My plan was to camp high on the historic ridge and descend to Traquair next day but gale force winds cast some doubt on my plans. I hoped the wind might ease off in the course of the day.

Before I left Melrose I was keen to take a look at the remains of Melrose Abbey, a magnificent red sandstone ruin on a lavish and grand scale. The Abbey is thought to be the burial place of Robert the Bruce's heart, marked with a commemorative carved stone plaque within the grounds. The rest of his body is buried in Dunfermline Abbey. An earlier monastery, at Old Melrose, about 3km east of the present Melrose Abbey, was founded by St Aidan of Lindisfarne shortly before his death in 651. St Cuthbert, whose ancient footsteps I had been following for the past couple of days, grew up nearby and trained there. In 662 Cuthbert was made prior of the monastery before being moved to Lindisfarne in Northumberland. King Kenneth MacAlpin eventually destroyed the old abbey in 839. Later, in the 12th century, Cistercian monks from Rievaulx Abbey in Yorkshire were asked by King David I to rebuild the Old Melrose Abbey but the monks chose to build it on better land in what we now know as Melrose. The east end of the Abbey was completed and dedicated in 1146 and other parts of the building were completed in the next 50 years. But the new Melrose Abbey was to have a pretty chequered future.

In 1322 the building was attacked and destroyed by the English army of Edward II but later rebuilt, largely through the generosity of Robert the Bruce. His heart, embalmed in lead, was later buried in the churchyard after it was returned from the Crusades with Lord Douglas in 1330. In 1385 the Abbey was once again burned down, this time by the army of Richard II of England, and then rebuilt, only to be destroyed once more during the War of the Rough Wooing. By 1556 the remaining monks complained that unless repairs were carried out the Abbey would not be able to continue to function. The last resident monk died at Melrose in about 1590. In 1610 part of the central portion of the nave of the Abbey was converted into Melrose parish church. This continued in use until replaced by a new church elsewhere in Melrose in 1810. Historic Scotland today looks after the remains of the Abbey.

Just over 400 metres high, the view from the easternmost of the Eildon Hills provides a fine panorama

Melrose to West Linton

Distance:	48km/30 miles.
Maps:	OS 1:50,000 sheets 73 and 72.
Public transport:	Buses to Melrose and West Linton from Edinburgh.
Accommodation:	Hotels, B&Bs and youth hostel in Melrose. Hotels and B&Bs in Galashiels, Traquair, Peebles and West Linton.
Route:	From Melrose follow Southern Upland Way signs around Galashiels to Yair, up past the Three Brethren and across the Minch Moor to Traquair.
	From Traquair follow Tweed Trail signs to Peebles and on over Hamilton Hill and the Meldons to Cloich Forest and West Linton.

I left the grounds of Melrose Abbey, collected my pack, and continued on my way without St Cuthbert. I was now following the route of the Southern Upland Way, one of Scotland's oldest long distance trails and the country's only official coast-to-coast route. It runs between Portpatrick in the west and Cockburnspath in the east and is 340km/212 miles in length, a considerable undertaking. Almost immediately the signposts directed me to the banks of the Tweed then easy riverside walking took me to Galashiels where I glimpsed, through a large plate glass window, rows of people working at their desks. The large window must have been a distraction to them – several waved to me and I waved back, smug in the knowledge that despite the rain and wind I wasn't shackled to a desk. The thought was curiously uplifting and I felt rejuvenated as I left the urban environment of Galashiels to climb over Hog Hill to Fairnilee House from where it was only a few minutes down to the tumultuous Tweed and the little car park and shelter at Yair.

It was a good spot to get out of the rain and grab some lunch before the climb up through the forest to the Three Brethren and the start of the Minch Moor.

The Three Brethren decorate the summit of Yair Hill and are on the route of Selkirk's Common Riding, an annual event that sees a cavalcade of horse riders go round the bounds, or marches, of Selkirk Burgh. The Brethren are three tall cairns, one of each standing within the districts of Selkirk Burgh, Yair and Bowhill. By now the wind had dropped from gale force to slightly mischievous and from time to time the sun broke through the racing clouds. I had been in good spirits since leaving Galashiels and it felt great to be up high for a while as I headed west along the broad path to the Broomy Law (any relationship to Glasgow's riverside Broomielaw, I wonder?) down into a fine little wooded glen and then uphill again towards the summit of Brown Knowe, where at 536m/1725ft a cairn marked the high point of my route between Kirk Yetholm and Edinburgh.

Just beyond Brown Knowe the Minch Moor track itself drops down the ridge between the Hangingshaw Burn and the Gruntly Burn, past some woods lower down and then into some other woods above Yarrowford. It's a route of considerable antiquity. Edward I came this way to conquer Scotland in 1296 and after the Battle of Philiphaugh James Graham, the Marquis of Montrose, crossed the route to Traquair House where he had hoped to find shelter. More recently, in 1931, a party of Scottish Youth Hostel Association officials crossed the Minch Moor to Broadmeadows to open Scotland's very first Youth Hostel. I camped in the forest, on a little patch of clumpy grass that was sheltered by trees on three sides. At times like this I tend to go onto automatic pilot – the well practised procedures of setting up camp and getting organised for the night have become so ingrained that I could probably do it with my eyes shut. Which is as well, for so often I find myself at this point of the day tired and thirsty and there have been times when that well-oiled routine has meant the difference between a comfortable night and a grim one. Especially in bad weather.

This evening was easy though. The pack comes off and I pull out the tent, leaving everything else I'll need for the night in the pack so I don't lose anything.

The Three Brethren – three huge cairns that are believed to date from the 16th century

When choosing a campsite I usually check the ground to see if there is a slope and if there is a slight one I tend to sleep with my feet at the higher end. The tent poles and pegs live in the same stuff sack as the tent so I pull them out and connect the pole ends together. I then stake out one end of the tent so it doesn't blow away if a gust of wind should catch it. The poles then go through the sleeves, I pull the tent out firmly to avoid any creases in the groundsheet, then stake out the corners and the guylines. Once the tent is erected it's time to pull out the sleep-mat, inflate it, and lay it inside the tent. Next comes the sleeping bag. I pull it out of its stuff sack, give it a shake or two to allow the air to get around the down and inflate it a bit then I lay it on the sleep-mat. Next job, before I finally get inside the tent, is to take my two water bladders and fill them. On this occasion there was a stream of fresh water only a few metres away so I filled the bladders using my mug to take the water from the shallow stream.

The disused railway line at Cardrona forms a picturesque approach to Peebles

I then usually take out my stove, pots, knife and spoon and anything else I might need for the night – a bag of food, a book, tomorrow's map and headtorch. By this time I'm usually ready to lie down. After a day's backpacking and all the bending down involved in putting up the tent I find my back tends to stiffen up, so it's great to lie down inside the tent for a few moments and just stretch it. Next comes the best moment of any camping experience. Lighting the stove, putting on a pot of water and anticipating the first brew. After that the evening passes in a fuzz of eating, drinking, reading and finally, sleeping…

Thankfully, the winds blew themselves out overnight. I woke to a sunny, but cool morning. It didn't take me long to drop down to Traquair where I was expecting a long road walk to Peebles, but a little sign marked Tweed Trails appeared on a gate.

It was the start of a lovely forest walk that climbed above the road and paralleled it almost all the way into Cardrona. But that wasn't all; another Tweed Trails sign pointed me across to the north bank of the river where a good footpath ran along the riverbank all the way into Peebles. I felt as though I had won the Lottery!

As part of the Land Reform (Scotland) Act of 2003, when Scotland was given access laws that have become the envy of the world, councils were asked to develop Core Path Networks around villages and towns. Tweed Trails is one such network and I was to make full use of it over the next couple of days. The Tweed Trails project has created an integrated network of paths in the Tweed catchment area. Local communities in Tweeddale and the British Horse Society (Scotland) started the project, which is now led by the Southern Uplands Partnership. In total the project has developed some 250km of paths, nearly all of which will be multi-use for walkers, cyclists and horse riders. Community paths around West Linton, Peebles, Innerleithen and Broughton and Biggar have been created alongside longer paths from Hawick to Newcastleton. The first Tweed Trail was officially opened by HRH Princess Anne in 2003.

There was something very satisfying about entering Peebles alongside the River Tweed, walking along a grassy bank onto the appropriately named Walkers' Haugh, as opposed to driving into the town in a car. I passed the pedestrian suspension bridge with the old bridge of Peebles and the spire of the Cross Kirk before me. Daffodils grew in abundance by the riverside and children played on the Tweed Green that runs up from the river. In contrast to Melrose, where I arrived wet and cold after a very rainy crossing of the Eildons, I felt fit and strong and relished the warmth and brightness of the sunshine that had made the day's walking so pleasant. But most of all I was hungry, and had a real notion for a Chinese nosh!

It was the great novelist Nigel Tranter who once described Peebles as the "comfortable, sonsy and still good-looking matron of the Borderland." I think I know what he meant. It is a comfortable kind of place, with a main street that still boasts independent shops rather than the who's who of retail chains that dominate so many High Streets the length and breadth of the UK. Indeed, the town has the distinction of being ranked as the Top Independent Retailing Town in Scotland, and second in the UK, for its range of independent shops and 'home town' identity in contrast to the ubiquitous 'cloned towns' predominant in other areas. On my recent Land's End to John O'Groats bike ride, my pal Hamish Telfer and I consistently followed new road layouts and roundabouts that led us to supermarket car parks. In the north-west of England in particular, it felt as though the hearts of towns had been torn out to make way for the great retail Gods of Tesco, Morrisons, Asda and the rest. In Peebles you get the comfortable feeling that such establishments might not be that welcome, certainly not in the town's wide High Street.

Nestled within an area of outstanding beauty and only 37km/23 miles south of Edinburgh, the Borders town of Peebles straddles the River Tweed, one of the best-known salmon fishing rivers in the world. In the nearby Glentress Forest an extensive network of mountain bike routes are waymarked through the trees and on the hills that surround the town footpaths and tracks date from the days of cattle droves and clan battles. Lower down the hill the Tweed Trails project looks after an integrated network of footpaths in the Tweed catchment area, including the riverbanks and forests around Peebles. Many of these routes have been used in the past by marching Romans, cattle drovers and the reivers who robbed and pillaged their way across the Border hills. A Royal Burgh since 1152 and the rule of King David I, Peebles has for many years been a market town cherished by locals and visitors alike. But there is some evidence to suggest that people lived here even before the 12th century. The Cross Kirk was built on the site where an early Christian stone cross was discovered in 1261 – it was the site of many pilgrimages up until the 17th century. The area on the west side of the Eddleston Water, where the remains of the Cross Kirk lie, is still referred to as the 'old town'.

Like many other Borders towns, Peebles has suffered at the hands of those involved in cross-border raids, from both north and south, particularly during the 14th and 16th centuries. Despite its status as a royal burgh, which enjoyed the occasional royal visit, the town was not walled until the 1570s but it was during the second half of the 19th century that Peebles really began to prosper, largely through sheep and the wool industry. The creation of the railway at this time allowed for greater movement of people and trade and the Peebles Hydro Hotel was opened in 1878, firmly establishing the town as a tourist destination.

Black Meldon lies west of Peebles and is seen here from its sister hill, White Meldon

It has never looked back. The 'comfortable, sonsy and still good-looking matron of the Borderland' description applies even to this day.

I set up my tent for the night in the town's campsite at Rosetta. My little backpackers' tent looked tiny sheltered beneath the overhanging branches of a great oak tree in the middle of a huge grassy slope normally full of caravans and motor campers. The isolation suited me fine. A wander back into town had me searching for a Chinese restaurant and moments later I was up to my ears in prawn crackers, noodles, spring onions and strips of chicken. A couple of Chinese beers helped me celebrate my progress…

Next morning, just beyond the campsite at Rosetta on the north side of Peebles, a Tweed Trails signpost pointed out a route over Hamilton Hill and down to Upper Kidston. "Meldons via Hamilton Hill and the Old Drove Road", it proclaimed. This was an area of Scotland that I was completely unfamiliar with, a lumpy, bumpy corner of the Borders where conifer forests potentially make the going difficult, so I was both delighted and relieved to see the Tweed Trails sign. I was even more delighted to find another sign that read "West Linton via the Old Drove Road". West Linton was my destination for the day. I had booked into the village's Gordon Arms for that night and if there was a signposted path, following an old drove road, all the way there then I wouldn't have to worry too much about navigating through dense forestry plantations. Even better, a signposted footpath suggested there might not be too much road walking to endure. My Ordnance Survey map had suggested a bewildering array of paths and tracks between here and West Linton but now that I knew I was on a waymarked route I reckoned I could just relax and enjoy the day. I set off up the hill in high spirits, the track rising gently before me and the wind at my back. For a change it wasn't raining and I took my time, looking back occasionally to enjoy the views of Peebles, nestled comfortably between its surrounding hills.

The track climbed gently up and away from Peebles and soon levelled out. Away to my right the busy A703 carried its daily commute of passengers towards Edinburgh, a road I had battled on a few weeks earlier on our End-to-End bike ride. I took some delight in the fact that today I didn't have to protect myself from buses, lorries and unforgiving car drivers and it wasn't long before the distant roar of traffic evaporated completely. I followed the track as it curved around Hamilton Hill the only sounds that reached my ears were the cries of sheep and the joyous outpouring of skylarks.

I followed a dry stone dyke to the bottom of the hill, crossed a footbridge and climbed uphill again beside a long, thin copse of trees. Ahead of me lay a farm track that led to the minor road that runs from Eddleston through the Meldons over to Lyne, the Old Post Road. It was a very quiet road, which was great because I had to walk along it for a while. At a car park and picnic area a car pulled in and a girl, dressed in hillwalking gear, asked if I knew the route up White Meldon.

The lonely farm of Upper Kidston is one of the few buildings passed on this section of the trail

I pointed roughly to my right and said "Up there, I think". She looked at me curiously. "Is there a path?" she asked. I began to explain that I didn't really know the area and there wasn't a path marked on the map, but it was less than a kilometre to the summit from the road. I was suddenly aware that I was mumbling but she stopped me in my tracks. "You're Cameron McNeish aren't you, off the Adventure Show"? I admitted I was. "Mmm, I thought you'd know the route up every hill", she blurted, before striding off in a cloud of exasperation.

I had little doubt she'd find the summit and I hoped she'd find the bronze age burial cairn that lies just north-west of the trig point. This whole area is a mass of burial cairns, standing stones, round cairns, timber cairns and henges and the entire summit of White Meldon, according to the Royal Commission for the Ancient and Historic Monuments of Scotland, forms the largest Iron Age hill fort in the county.

The village church in the picturesque community of West Linton

Four separate defensive lines can apparently be traced, though not all remain intact. Another hill fort lies nearby on the summit of Black Meldon, just across the valley, and slightly north there are two more substantial hill forts on Harehope Hill.

Half a kilometre further along the road a signpost suggested I turn left and then immediately right along a track that led through the forest and then up to the farmhouse at Stewarton. Just beyond the buildings a three-way signpost indicated another track, which I followed past a ruined barn, through a gate and into the green embrace of the Cloich Forest. The path climbed uphill through the forest for almost a kilometre, crossing a forest ride, before levelling out and then dropping gently to a large clearing at Courhope. More signposts kept me on the correct forest track and 20 minutes or so later I was free of the trees and exposed to the wide views to the west, down the length of the Flemington Burn, and north towards Hag Law and Wether Law and the isolated Fingland bothy.

A lovely path carried me uphill above the Fingland Burn between Drum Maw and the long rounded ridge of Hag Law before entering a narrow strip of woodland where I picked up a gorse-lined path that descended to Romannobridge, a small village I knew of from the writings of one of my favourite novelists, Andrew Greig. A footpath, which appeared obvious on the map but failed to materialise in reality, should have followed the Lyne Water to West Linton, but despite searching I couldn't find it. Instead I discovered another Tweed Trails sign, this time marked as "West Linton via Broomlee Hill". Fantastic! Various paths, tracks and short sections of road, all well signposted, took me past the radio masts on the brow of Broomlee Hill and down to the B7059 and the short walk into West Linton where I checked into the Gordon Arms for the night. The next day would be a big one and I reckoned I needed a good sleep and the staying power benefit of a full Scottish breakfast in the morning.

When looking for accommodation in West Linton at the start of my walk I noticed the community website made a show of admitting that no great Scottish events took place here. However, it must have been quite a place in the past for it stands on the crossing of drove roads. The north/south route passes through the Pentland Hills at the Cauldstane Slap and on to the south through the village and the east/west route, between Edinburgh and the south-west, passes just north of the village.

The Cauldstane Slap (a 'slap' is a pass) route, referred to on Roy's map of 1755 as the Road to Queensferry, would have seen cattle and sheep brought from the highlands via Falkirk, and then down through West Linton to Peebles and St Mary's Loch before crossing the border into England.

In his excellent book *The Drove Roads of Scotland*, A.R.B.Haldane shows it as being the only route by which cattle were taken from north of the central belt to markets further south. While it is unlikely to be the sole route, it must have been of considerable importance and surely must have had tens of thousands of cattle travelling along it every year. In the reverse direction, sheep from the Linton markets were driven to the Highlands, probably about 30,000 annually. It is also known, as many drove roads are, as the Thieves Road as it must have been used by

West Cairn Hill is worth a short diversion with its panoramic view of Edinburgh and the route ahead

a fair number of cattle thieves as well as legitimate traders. As late as 1600 there is a record of a party of Scotts and Armstrongs stealing 80 cattle and taking them southwards along this path, leaving several people dead and wounded in their wake.

The Gordon Arms has been an inn since it was built in 1654 and the bar was busy as I settled myself in the corner with a substantial bar meal and my maps. An elderly man sat beside me and asked where I was heading for and it wasn't long before we were deep in conversation about the area. He was a fount of knowledge, and he reckoned my best route over the Pentlands to Balerno would be to follow an old Roman Road, which ran parallel to the A702, to Carlops, then take the track past the Bore Stane and down into Balerno and the start of the Water of Leith walk into Edinburgh. He also suggested I look out for the nearby Medwyn House, which apparently stands on the site of a former coaching inn called Bridgehouse Inn. It's claimed the innkeeper was a pal of Robert Burns but was never at home when the bard came to visit. In frustration, Burns scratched a message on the inn's window – *"Honest Graham, aye the same, never to be found at hame."*

West Linton to Edinburgh

Distance:	32km/20 miles.
Ascent:	300m/1000ft approx.
Maps:	OS 1:50,000 sheets 72, 65 and 66.
Public transport:	Buses from Edinburgh to West Linton. Edinburgh is a major hub with good bus, rail and air links to the rest of the UK and abroad.
Accommodation:	Hotel and B&Bs in West Linton. Wide selection of accommodation of all kinds in Edinburgh.
Route:	Leave West Linton on the minor road to the golf course but turn right on the road and then track signposted to Carlops. Take the track past North Esk Reservoir and the Bore Stane to Listonshiels. Continue on minor roads to Balerno to pick up the Water of Leith Walkway to Slateford (or continue into Edinburgh city centre if you wish).

After breakfast next morning, a stiff climb from West Linton took me towards the Cairn Muir and the Cauldstane Slap, but well before I reached the Muir a minor road ran off to the right. This eventually metamorphosed into a track that followed the line of the Roman Road past Linton Muir and Hartside and all the way into Carlops. From there, another track ran uphill past Fairliehope to the North Esk Reservoir from where a footpath continued north-east, past Cock Rig and the Bore Stane and down the other side to the farm at Listonshiels. From there a series of minor roads took me into Balerno and the start of the Water of Leith footpath that was to take me all the way into the heart of Edinburgh.

The Pentland Hills are the first high ground crossed by walkers. On a fine summer's evening, this is the view to East Cairn Hill

Flowing for 38km/24 miles from its source in the Pentland Hills, the Water of Leith winds its way through Balerno, Currie, Juniper Green, Colinton, Slateford, Roseburn and Dean Village into the heart of auld Edinburgh, before continuing through Stockbridge, Canonmills and Bonnington to the Firth of Forth at Leith. Once Edinburgh's industrial heartland, the valley was host to over 70 mills harnessing the power of the water to produce paper, fabric, and flour with the river mouth supporting a vibrant dock and boatbuilding industry. Today the river is home to a wide diversity of plants and animals from wild garlic and orchids to brown trout, heron, kingfisher and otter, and can be explored on foot or bike along the 21km/13-mile Water of Leith Walkway. The Water of Leith Conservation Trust works to conserve and enhance the river and its banks and it does a fantastic job.

In the heart of Edinburgh, the Water of Leith goes through the historic Dean Village

In operation since 1988, the Conservation Trust was the first river charity to be established in Scotland and has developed an excellent Visitor Centre at Slateford, just below the Union Canal. There was a touch of serendipity about this. When I was initially planning this route I had little idea of how I would get out of Edinburgh and start making my way west to pick up a route that would take me north. Then I remembered the Union and Forth and Clyde Canals. The Union Canal runs from Fountainbridge in Edinburgh to Falkirk, where it meets the Forth and Clyde Canal, which runs into Glasgow. I had my answer. Two or three days canal towpath walking would take me across the Central Belt towards the start of the West Highland Way and the long trail north. But then I heard about the nascent John Muir Way...

CHAPTER 2

EDINBURGH TO MILNGAVIE

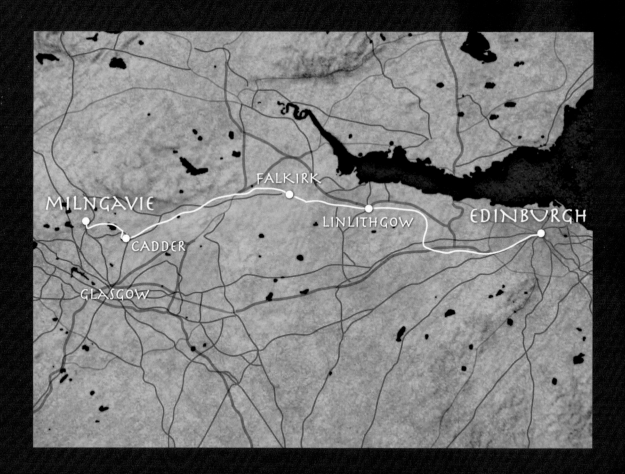

Start:	Edinburgh (Water of Leith Conservation Trust Visitor Centre, Slateford, GR223708).
Finish:	Milngavie.
Distance:	82km/51 miles approx.
Maps:	This section is covered (in walking order) by Ordnance Survey 1:50,000 Landranger sheets 66, 65 and 64.
Public transport:	Edinburgh and Glasgow are major hubs with good bus, rail and air links to the rest of the UK and abroad. Excellent bus and train links between Edinburgh and Glasgow via Linlithgow and Falkirk. For more information on public transport phone 0871 200 22 33 or go to www.travelinescotland.com.
Accommodation:	Very wide range of accommodation in both Edinburgh and Glasgow. Hotels and B&Bs in Linlithgow, Falkirk, Kilsyth, Kirkintilloch and Milngavie.
Route:	Follow the towpath of the Union Canal from Slateford all the way to the Falkirk Wheel. Pick up the towpath of the Forth and Clyde Canal here and follow it to Cadder (GR 616722). From here follow the route to Milngavie via Balmore outlined in the text.

Additional route information
Much of the route is described in Hamish Brown's book *From the Pennines to the Highlands*. Also useful are the British Waterways Scotland website at www.britishwaterways.co.uk/scotland, and www.thefalkirkwheel.co.uk

General information
For more information on accommodation, visitor attractions etc, go to www.visitedinburgh.com, www.linlithgow.com, www.visitscottishheartlands.com and www.visitglasgow.com.

Looking east from the Campsie Fells to the route through Scotland's central belt

Edinburgh to Milngavie

through the Central Belt from East to West

You can't give a walking route the title of the Scottish National Trail and not have it visit the capital city, Edinburgh. The Water of Leith makes a delightful climax to the first section of the trail, and if you intend walking the whole route of the Gore-Tex Scottish National Trail then this will be your one and only opportunity of spending a night in a city, and for outdoors folk in particular, Edinburgh is a very special city.

Often described as the Athens of the North, Edinburgh throbs and thrums with historical connections. The castle, the walled stronghold that dominates the city centre, is on a site which has been fortified for over 3,000 years and has been a seat of royalty, headquarters of the Sheriff of Edinburgh, a military garrison and the repository of the nation's crown jewels. The contrasting medieval Old Town and the Georgian New Town were listed as a UNESCO World Heritage Site in 1995 and of course Edinburgh was the centre of the Scottish Enlightenment, a rich cultural period in the 18th century that saw a massive outpouring of intellectual and scientific accomplishments covering a diverse range of specialist fields including philosophy, engineering, medicine, geology and the arts. It was a period that produced such outstanding thinkers as David Hume, Adam Smith, Robert Burns, Adam Ferguson and James Hutton, and dozens of others.

What excites me most about Edinburgh is the fact that it is the only city in the UK that has a mountain within its city boundaries.

Robert Louis Stevenson once described Arthur's Seat as: "a hill for magnitude, a mountain in virtue of its bold design". And bold it certainly is. Rising to a height of just 250m/822 feet it may lack the drama and status of a Munro but within its city centre location it is both dramatic and impressive with wide-ranging views over the city and across the Firth of Forth towards Fife and the distant highland line. The ascent of this "bold mountain" is a proper hill-walk!

Arthur's Seat was formed as part of a volcano system some 350 million years ago. More recently, probably about two million years ago, a glacier moving in a rough west to east direction exposing the rocky cliffs of what we now call Salisbury Crags, eroded it into the familiar shape it is today. The impressive crags form the backdrop to Scotland's modern parliament buildings at Holyrood. But probably the most impressive fact about Edinburgh is this – the number of visitors attracted to Edinburgh for the annual Edinburgh Festival is roughly equal to the settled population of the city. The city attracts over one million overseas visitors a year, making it the second most visited tourist destination in the United Kingdom. A million visitors can't all be wrong.

I have a huge personal fondness for Edinburgh. I love the atmosphere of the Old Town and the gentility of the New Town, I love the coffee shops of Bruntsfield and Morningside and I can lose myself in the historic wynds and lanes of the Royal Mile, but given all that I was glad to start walking from the Water of Leith Visitor Centre at Slateford and take my first steps along the towpath of the Union Canal. I was heading west, and, despite my fondness for the capital, west is where my heart lies.

In May 2010, I took part in the annual TGO (The Great Outdoors) Challenge, a two-week cross-Scotland backpacking event. I started at Inverie in Knoydart and the plan was to walk across Scotland to finish at St Cyrus, near Montrose on the east coast. It was great to meet friends, both old and new, on the ferry crossing between Mallaig and Inverie and there was a real party atmosphere, a shared sense of anticipation, but as soon as I began walking I felt, instinctively, that something was wrong.

Fellow Challengers had taken the decision to stop at the pub in Inverie and I had to fight off an overwhelming desire to linger with them.

The Scottish Parliament building in Edinburgh

I didn't really want a beer, nor was I that keen on socialising so early on the Challenge, but I definitely felt out of sorts. I was walking with my wife and brother-in-law and it wasn't until we crossed over the Mam Meadail, the first divide of our walk between Inverie and St Cyrus, that I suddenly realised what was niggling me. Dropping down from the high pass towards Sourlies, with Sgurr na Ciche and Ben Aden looming over us, an awareness of what lay ahead of us unexpectedly hit me. Curiously it wasn't the fact that we had over 300 kilometres of mountain terrain, tracks and footpaths to negotiate, rather that I sensed, somewhere in my being, that we were going the 'wrong' way. We were walking east against all my natural inclinations, and the power of those inclinations almost stopped me in my tracks. I was leaving my beloved west behind...

The sun rises in the east and sets in the west. Celtic traditions have it that beyond the western sea, off the edges of all maps, lay the Otherworld, or Afterlife. The great religions of the world all point in that direction – the West represents movement toward the Buddha or enlightenment. Ancient Egyptians believed that the Goddess Amunet, protector of the Pharaoh, was a personification of the West. The American West is a symbol of freedom – 'go west, young man, and grow up with the country'. I'm not sure I had ever thought of this before. I had no idea I was in thrall to the West to such an extent, but later that night, as Raymond and Gina stayed in our camp near Sourlies I took myself off up the hillside and considered my loss.

As I thought about it I realised that all my best backpacking trips have been in the direction of west, or north. I've always preferred the west coast of the USA to the east; I've travelled extensively on the west coast of Ireland but very little in the east; I really don't know the east of England at all but I'm passionate about the Lake District, Wales and the West Country. For a number of years I lived in Aberdeen but I couldn't settle in that east coast city. All my inclinations point west, and I'm not really sure why. Perhaps it's something to do with Celtic genes? But now I was heading west out of Edinburgh and after that I'd be heading north, to the most north-westerly point on the Scottish mainland. It felt as though I was going home…

The excellent Water of Leith Information Centre, run by the Water of Leith Conservation Trust, is situated in a renovated schoolhouse on the banks of the Water of Leith itself. An informative exhibition tells the story of the river and there's a cafe selling teas, coffees and snacks. There's a gift shop too, selling books and souvenirs. Just beyond the Centre an aqueduct carries the Union Canal over the river and beyond it a bridge carries the main Edinburgh to Glasgow rail line across.

The Union Canal is an amazing feat of engineering, and good news for walkers. Often described as a 'contour canal' it follows the 73-metre/240ft contour for almost its entire length, between Fountainbridge, in the centre of Edinburgh and Falkirk. That means no hills, and virtually no canal locks, although a couple of new locks have been created just before the unique Falkirk Wheel. Instead of using locks the canal maintains its level by embankments, cuttings and major aqueducts.

Originally known as the Edinburgh and Glasgow Union Canal, the canal was designed by Hugh Baird who oversaw the engineering work while the canal was being built between 1818 and 1822. Navvies, many of them from Ireland, made up the bulk of the construction workers and two of them later achieved a certain level of notoriety. Their names were Burke and Hare, serial murderers who sold the bodies of their victims to Dr Robert Knox, a private anatomy lecturer who dissected the bodies for his students.

The canal was originally used for the transportation of coal, but the rapid growth of the railways had a dire effect on trade and the canal just couldn't compete with the faster mode of transport. It closed for commercial use in the 1930s and went into a long period of decline, which saw the locks at Falkirk, where the Union Canal met the Forth and Clyde Canal, filled in and built over. Thankfully, British Waterways Scotland had other plans for this important aspect of Scotland's industrial heritage. National Lottery funds in the form of the Millennium Link were used to regenerate both the Forth and Clyde and Union Canals as part of the Millennium celebrations in 2000 and the Falkirk Wheel, a unique boat lift, was completed in 2002 to provide a link between the two canals and allow boats to travel all the way from Bowling, on the Clyde near Glasgow, to Edinburgh and vice versa. And as I was about to discover, the towpaths of the two canals make a fantastic and straightforward walking route between Glasgow and Edinburgh.

The canals also make up a substantial part of the new John Muir Way, which will eventually run from Dunbar in East Lothian, the birthplace of the 19th century naturalist, all the way across Scotland to Helensburgh, just across the River Clyde from where Muir left the shores of Scotland to migrate with his family to Wisconsin in the US. At the moment the John Muir Way finishes in South Queensferry, just below the Forth Bridges, but plans from Scottish Natural Heritage and the Central Scotland Green Network will see the route extended west along the shore of the River Forth to Bo'ness where it turns south to link with the Union Canal at Linlithgow. It follows the canal towpath to Falkirk and then deviates a couple of times along sections of the Roman Antonine Wall before returning to the canal at the Falkirk Wheel.

The Forth and Clyde Canal provides an unexpectedly attractive way to traverse Scotland's industrial Central Belt

It then more or less follows the Forth and Clyde Canal as far as Banknock where it leaves the canal path to trace the Antonine Wall again to Twechar where, once again, it returns to the canal. It leaves the canal permanently at Kirkintilloch and takes a more northerly route, following an old railway line to Milton of Campsie and Strathblane where it joins the West Highland Way to Gartness before heading west to Croftamie and, skirting north of the Cameron Muir, to Drumglas, Balloch, and over the Auchendennan and Bannachra Muirs to journey's end at Helensburgh. It's hoped to have the new route finished by the time of the centenary of John Muir's death in 2014.

Once the route is completed and signposted various sections of it, particularly the sections along the Antonine Wall at Falkirk and between Banknock and Twechar, will provide welcome alternative routes for those using the Gore-Tex Scottish National Trail. I must confess that I was delighted when I heard the news that the John Muir Way is to be extended to become Scotland's second coast-to-coast long distance walking route, the first being the Southern Upland Way, for I've campaigned for long enough to have the name of John Muir recognised more in the land of his birth. He was an astonishing character who left behind a wealth of books outlining his adventures and philosophies about nature and our relationship to it. Indeed, Muir became the only Scot that I know of to feature on an American coin when Governor Arnold Schwarzenegger of California decided that John Muir and Yosemite should feature on a new California State Quarter. "John Muir has been a role model to generations of Californians and to conservationists around the world. He taught us to be active and to enjoy – but at the same time protect – our parks, our beaches, and our mountains", said the Governor as he announced selection of the John Muir-Yosemite Design for the California State Quarter.

John Muir, of course, emigrated to the USA from Dunbar at the age of 11 and later became one of the father figures of the world conservation movement. In 2000 President Bill Clinton made him a Man of the Millennium. It seems as though this generation has grasped the prophet's unique insights into the natural world and man's relationship to it and as a result more words have been written about John Muir in the past few years than ever before. Thankfully, Muir's voice still echoes down through the decades and while others mimic his battle cries, and articulate his ecological theology, no-one has successfully imitated his primal zest in enthusing politicians about the values of wildness and the importance of preserving it.

I regularly give an audio-visual presentation about John Muir and I always finish with the story of Henry Bradford Loomis. Loomis was a young Seattle attorney who went on an expedition with John Muir to Alaska in 1890. For the first couple of weeks Loomis was downright miserable – he complained of the cold, lack of shelter and the bitter, piercing wind, but Muir by all accounts was in his element.

In time a metamorphosis took place in Loomis' mind. He began to see beyond his own discomforts and grumbles, he began to see, through Muir's passion and enthusiasm, that he was in a wondrous place, and soon he was rhapsodising in typical John Muir style. John Muir was a catalyst in the life of that young attorney. Loomis caught something of Muir's enthusiasm and eagerness for life and all its fullness, but more importantly, he learned that the natural world was a place of infinite beauty. In the company of the prophet, Loomis encountered the sacred in those northern mountain landscapes, he experienced fresh insights and understandings of himself and the world in which he lived.

My great hope is that Muir's transcendent vision of the natural world will have the same effect on people today that it had on Henry Loomis. Perhaps this clarion call, coming down through the decades, will teach us that one of the main values of experiencing our wild places is not simply about conquering or collecting ticked lists of mountains or even the economic advantages that walking or climbing brings to rural communities. These things are all fine and perfectly valid, but the vital lesson that John Muir brings to us today is that mankind is not the owner, or in charge of the biotic community, but an equal partner in it. That knowledge brings a simple responsibility – to look after the planet that sustains us.

I've often described John Muir as The Prophet, and probably no words of his ring so true today as these: "Thousands of tired, nerve-shaken, over-civilised people are beginning to find out that going to the mountains is going home. That wildness is a necessity; and that mountain parks and reservations are useful not only as fountains of timber and irrigating rivers, but as fountains of life." And as a corollary to that, I believe these words of Edward Abbey, another wilderness champion, are just as important; "Wilderness complements and compliments civilisation. I might say that the existence of wilderness is also a compliment to civilisation. Any society that feels itself too poor to afford the preservation of wilderness, is not worthy of the name of civilisation". We're not talking about wilderness in the context of the Union or Forth and Clyde Canals but later on, as the Gore-Tex Scottish National Trail makes its way through the northern highlands, we'll find ourselves in landscapes that are as near to wilderness as dammit. And in a Scotland where we are losing our wild land areas at a very worrying rate, largely because of large-scale windfarms and miles upon miles of bulldozed, high level tracks, it might be wise for us to remember the words of both Muir and Abbey.

From Slateford the Union Canal takes a rather aloof and meandering line through Wester Hailes and Hermiston, crosses majestically over the busy A720 Ring Road (by aqueduct) and, surprisingly quickly, carries you into a green and leafy rural environment just beyond Hermiston House, a two-storey baronial mansion that began life as the dower house for the Riccarton Estate in 1633. It was remodelled by the architect William Burn who lived there in the mid-19th century and was restored and modernised by Esmé Gordon in 1955. It's now used as the residence for the Principal of the nearby Heriot-Watt University. The constant roar of aircraft, taking off and landing at the nearby Edinburgh Airport, may have spoiled the rural tranquility a little but already, after just a short distance, the calm of the canal was having an effect on me. As I approached Ratho one or two houseboats passed by, the owners snuggled down in the stern by the tiller, keeping the long boat in a straight line. Every time I see one of these houseboats I long to try one out, to have a holiday on one, negotiating the peaceful canals, drifting along quietly and unobtrusively, letting the world go by. It definitely seems like life in the slow lane, the perfect antidote to the stressful lives so many of us lead.

I stopped at the Bridge Inn in Ratho for an early lunch. The inn had just been named as Scottish Pub of the Year by the Catering in Scotland Excellence Awards, so I couldn't very well pass it by. After feeding the inner man, I noticed one of the houseboats was being tied up alongside. A bearded and pony-tailed man jumped on to the quay and I asked him if he was tying up for the day. We quickly got into conversation and I learned that people who live on houseboats are called 'liveaboards' and that there are currently about 15,000 of them living on the canals of Britain. That's a sizeable community, a sub-culture of people who have left the rat-race and have chosen a life that by its very nature tends to be 'green'. I suggested you could describe such folk as 'eco river gypsies'. "I guess you could call us that," he said with a broad grin. "The truth is we don't have a lot of choice.

You have to be environmentally conscious when you live on a houseboat. You can't leave taps running, 12-volt batteries as your sole means of power require a certain amount of care, and I use a Morso wood-burning stove for heat in the winter. We certainly use red diesel but more and more folk are moving over to biofuels."

I asked him if he berthed at Ratho permanently but he shook his head vigorously. "I have what you call a 'continuous cruiser' licence. That means I can only stay in one place for a maximum of 14 days, but that suits me. I bought this boat because I wanted to move around, to travel, and that's what I do, between Edinburgh and Bowling on the other side of Glasgow. I've been living on the boat for three years and it suits me just fine." We shook hands and he went off for a beer while I turned west again. I wanted to reach Linlithgow by evening and that was still about 21km away, but I took some consolation in the fact that I wouldn't have any hills to climb. You can't get much flatter than a canal towpath.

In the course of the next few kilometres, which took me through the West Lothian towns of Broxburn and Winchburgh and the red man-made mountains that dominate the landscape, the number of people using the canal towpath and the canal itself amazed me. There was a steady stream of houseboats and the occasional canoeist and I met dog walkers, power walkers, cyclists and joggers, all enjoying the relative tranquillity of this watercourse that weaves its way quietly through the countryside, often only a short step away from roads that were hidden by trees, that toweres over the canal and towpath creating long, green tunnels. By the time I reached Linlithgow, I had become a fully paid-up member of the 'Union Canal fan club'. It's worth mentioning the red shale pit bings that dominate the landscape between Broxburn and Winchburgh. Sometimes referred to as the Five Sisters of West Lothian, these man-made mountains are waste heaps from the oil shale industry that was centred largely on this part of Scotland. The main products of the industry, pioneered by James 'Paraffin' Young, were crude oil, which could be fractionally distilled to produce naphtha, burning oil, cleaning oil and lubricating oil as well as ammonia. Production peaked in 1913 at 3.25 million tonnes but oil shale extraction ended in 1962 as other source materials emerged and the seams were worked out.

Boats of the Forth & Clyde Society moored on the canal close to Glasgow

While many of the original bings have been removed, Scottish Natural Heritage has become more and more aware that the remaining waste heaps represent interesting and potentially unique habitats which can, with time, develop into a valuable natural heritage resource. The following statement is from one of their own Information and Advisory Notes: "The nature conservation importance of bings lies in the fact that they often represent small pockets of a highly distinctive environment, thus providing specialised ecological niches. For this reason bings may be worthy of protection. Many old sites which have been colonised naturally show interesting botanical features and may also be important habitats for wildlife.

Bings may also have an earth science interest in that some may show evidence of soil formation. The waste material in a bing is essentially crushed rock which may be considered as a soil parent material. This, combined with the known age and history of most bings and any natural vegetation which has become established, could provide a useful study site for the processes which act on rock to begin soil formation." Who would have believed it? The word 'bing' incidentally, comes from the same source as the Gaelic word 'beinn' or 'ben' meaning a hill.

As I walked along the broad canal paths I had been dipping into Hamish Brown's excellent book, *From the Pennines to the Highlands.* His descriptions of the canals and the towns and villages they pass through, were detailed and quite fascinating, although he did suggest that stretches of the canal suffered from a surface layer of slime and litter, and that this section near Broxburn, in particular, had more than its fair share of rubbish dumped in the water. I'm delighted to report that things have changed dramatically in the 20 years since Hamish's book was published. Indeed, the lack of litter was something that constantly amazed me, as was the quality of the towpath surface. There's little doubt that British Waterways Scotland has reversed years of neglect and revitalised Scotland's canals, transforming them into important national assets. They really deserve to be better known by outdoor folk.

I had noted that Hamish also made a point of saying that there were very few eating establishments in Lithlithgow, and after a long day of over 40km of walking, albeit all on the flat, I had the appetite of a horse. I hoped the culinary situation had changed. My host in the little Bed and Breakfast I had booked into assured me I wouldn't starve. "There's plenty o' carry-oot places", she told me, "and ye're very welcome to bring something back here wi' ye. But we've got Indian, Chinese and Italian restaurants and at least three chippies!" I opted for the Italian, a wonderful restaurant called Bar Leo, and a magnificent pasta dish with tomato sauce and Italian spiced sausage, washed down with a couple of glasses of chilled pinot grigio. Backpacking doesn't always have to be about roughing it and as I've claimed many a time, any fool can be uncomfortable.

I had the wind and rain in my face next morning but I was still in a bit of a honeymoon phase. Canal walking like this was relatively new to me, still a novel experience, and I found that with no navigation issues to worry about I could wander along the flat towpath and simply allow my mind to roam, free as a cloud, and it did. As I've mentioned I was even able to read a book as I walked. The miles passed easily; over the 250m-long Avon Aqueduct, the second longest in the UK, through a relatively short industrialised area in Polmont, with the flaming torches of the Grangemouth petro-chemical works in the distance, and then back into the leafy channel of the canal as it made its way through Falkirk, partly through a long tunnel that was carved out of the rock below the district today known as Glen Village. The 220-metre tunnel is known locally as the 'Dark Tunnel', and I can understand why, although there is electric lighting in it. Indeed, the lights have an amazing effect on the water surface, casting a reflection of the rock-hewn roof of the tunnel, giving the impression that you are looking down, through crystal clear water, to rocky depths.

Beyond the tunnel a long straight section of canal leads to a couple of comparatively new locks, the only ones on the whole length of the Union Canal, and beyond them the canal runs through another tunnel before leading onto a long aqueduct that appears to suddenly stop in mid-air. It's an astonishing sight but even more astonishing is the brilliant engineering landmark that is known as the Falkirk Wheel. I wandered down the pathway beside it, aware that my jaw was probably dropping in surprise at what lay before me. The Falkirk Wheel is a rotating boat lift and is the only one of its kind in the world. Essentially it lifts canal boats from the Forth and Clyde Canal to the higher level of the Union Canal, about 24 metres, without having to use any locks, the usual method of transporting boats to different levels. The two canals were previously connected by a series of 11 locks but these had fallen into disuse in the 1930s and were eventually filled in. I joined a group of camera clicking tourists at the foot of the wheel as a boat made its way along the aqueduct above us. The end of the aqueduct then opened directly into the upper of the two gondolas that carry the boats. After a few minutes the great wheel began to rotate very slowly, bringing the gondola with its boat down into a circular basin below. A lock from the nearby Forth and Clyde Canal accesses this basin, a colourful scene with a flotilla of boats moored around its banks.

A marvel of modern engineering, the Falkirk Wheel is the essential link between the Union Canal and the Forth and Clyde Canal

The Wheel itself is 35 metres high, and each gondola contains 300 tonnes of water. Because the gondolas are always in balance (because boats displace their own weight of water) moving them takes surprisingly little power. Someone suggested it all works on the output of half a dozen motor scooters! It really is a modern wonder, and it sits cheek by jowl with one of the wonders of the Scottish ancient world – the Antonine Wall. A footpath from the Wheel's visitor centre takes you to the Rough Castle Roman Fort, one of the best places to get a feel for what the Wall would have been like. The Antonine Wall was only in use for about 20 years.

Maybe the Romans didn't fancy our weather, or maybe the midges were too much for them, but whatever the reason, they didn't hang around in Scotland for too long before relocating to the garrisons of Hadrian's Wall in Northumberland. The Antonine Wall only took about two years to build, and that's pretty impressive given that it's a good 60km in length, running from Bo'ness on the River Forth to Old Kilpatrick in the west.

The Romans never did conquer what we know today as Scotland, but the wall was used to control the flow of people and goods and probably had a military function in protecting the Roman-held land to the south from any attack from the northern Caledonians. Just north of Rough Castle you can still see the line of a series of pits, which would have been lined with sharp stakes and covered over with brushwood, designed to thwart any attack on the wall itself from the north. The wall would have been built of stone and turf and dates to the middle second century AD.

I felt curiously reluctant to leave the ancient wall and the ultra-modern Falkirk Wheel behind and part of me was tempted to try to follow the line of the Antonine Wall west rather than return to the canal towpaths, but I was running short of time – I had spent over two hours here and needed to move on if I was going to reach Kilsyth that night. It was still 15km away. From there I had an easy 22km walk next day, from Kilsyth to Cadder on the Forth and Clyde canal, and a little link route that would take me north through Balmore to Milngavie and the start of the West Highland Way.

Easy walking took me past more moored houseboats then past the first locks of the Forth and Clyde Canal. Designed by the eminent civil engineer John Smeaton and completed in 1790, the Forth and Clyde Canal crossed the Scottish lowlands at their narrowest part, and ran for 56km, providing a route for sea-going vessels between the Firth of Clyde and the Firth of Forth via a short stretch of the River Carron near Grangemouth in the east. Between 1789 and 1803 the canal was used for trials of William Symington's steamboats, culminating in the *Charlotte Dundas*, the "first practical steamboat". The canal subsequently became a major route for Clyde puffers, many of which were constructed at Bowling, but like the Union Canal it fell into disuse until National Lottery funds were used to regenerate it as part of the Millennium celebrations in 2000.

As I wandered along this natural lung of Scotland's central belt I found it difficult to believe I was passing through areas that I had always associated with large and sprawling housing developments with all their associated social problems – Bonnybridge, Dennyloanhead and Cumbernauld – but in reality I was walking along a very green rural lane, sequestered from the built-up areas and busy roads by bands of trees and fields. Earlier I had spotted a kingfisher, the last bird I had expected to see on a Scottish urban canal, and I had lost count of the number of herons and dippers I had seen. Both canals form a long and elongated wildlife reserve. At one point I passed below the M80, a road that I used to drive along several times a week. It wasn't until I checked my map that I was aware I had passed under one of the busiest roads in Scotland.

I left the canal at Kilsyth, close to Auchinstarry Quarry where I used to go rock climbing many years ago. It's an old dolerite quarry that's been landscaped to provide an excellent rock climbing area with a number of good routes, mostly in the extreme grades. It lies between the village of Croy and Kilsyth, which claims to be the place where the sport of curling began. The town certainly had the world's very first curling club, which used to play on the frozen loch at the nearby Colzium Estate. It was about a kilometre or so into the town and I felt it appropriate to see if I could embrace a bygone era of weary travellers and arduous coach journeys and try for a room in the Coachman Hotel. After studiously checking the bookings register and counting the room keys on the wall, the receptionist suggested she could probably squeeze me in for the night. It was a good performance – I suspect I was the only person staying.

Certainly there were no other guests around as I enjoyed an excellent breakfast and set out once again, this time for the short hop down the canal to Kirkintilloch, at one time a 'dry' town. The sale of alcohol was banned from 1923 until 1967 thanks to the strong influence in the town of the temperance movement. In the 1960s there was a plan to develop the inner city areas of Glasgow so large numbers of Glaswegians were relocated into 'overspill' areas like Kirkintilloch, Livingston and Cumbernauld, and those Glaswegians didn't like the idea of a town with no pubs. A folk song of the time claimed:

"In Kirkintilloch there's nae pubs and I'm sure ye'll wonder why; my brither and me we went for a spree and drank the pubs aw dry, aw dry; we drank the pubs aw dry".

The leafy suburb of Cadder was the end of the line for my walk along the Forth and Clyde Canal. I had spent a considerable amount of time pondering over maps, trying to find a good link between the canal and the start of the West Highland Way in Milngavie but it wasn't until I had been walking along the canal towpath reading Hamish Brown's book *From the Pennines to the Highlands* that I found the answer. Hamish had discovered a lovely little route that crosses the River Kelvin, before making its way over the beautifully situated Balmore Golf Club to Bardowie where a series of narrow minor roads led into Milngavie, the starting point of the West Highland Way. I felt a little sad having to leave the canal behind. I had hugely enjoyed the easy walking from Edinburgh and had been genuinely impressed by the Falkirk Wheel and the excellent condition of the canals and the towpaths, a real resource that should be much better known. I hope the Gore-Tex Scottish National Trail might help spread the news of the wonderful job being done by British Waterways Scotland.

I was now heading north, past Cadder Church, set in its leafy glade, and down a narrow lane towards the Keir Golf Course. I always feel a tad uncomfortable about walking across golf courses, even though it is perfectly legal to do so in Scotland provided you act responsibly. In this instance I didn't have to worry. A narrow footpath with trees on both sides took me alongside one of the fairways as far as the River Kelvin where a footbridge should take you across the river to another footpath that led to Balmore. I found the footbridge easily enough, but it was locked up and a sign proclaimed it closed until further notice. It should be reopened by the time you read this, but if it isn't just follow the rerouting outlined below.

The diversion took me east along the banks of the Kelvin to the village of Torrance, from where a pavement by the A807 brought me back to Balmore and Hamish's original route. A signpost indicated a coffee shop and I discovered a real little treasure of a place. The Balmore Coach House has a secondhand book shop, a wide variety of craft products and a charming coffee shop. Just the place for a break. The friendly lady who was serving told me something of the history of the place. It was established 30 years ago when the Balmore Trust was set up to distribute any profits from the business. It was hoped that the Coach House would provide a meeting place for those in the area who wanted to do something about the huge divide between the 'haves' and the 'have-nots', both at home and abroad. Today the Coach House and its Fairtrade tearoom is still a popular meeting place and the shop is jam-packed with a huge range of unique crafts, clothes and foods from all around the world.

On the other side of the A807, Glenorchard Road climbs a hill and takes a sharp left turn before turning right again into the grounds of Balmore Golf Club. Our route goes behind the clubhouse and follows a footpath down towards a little bridge over the culvert that contains the Branziet Burn. Cross the bridge and continue on the path around the edge of the fairway to the 17th hole where a footpath comes in from the left beside the stream. Follow it along a bank towards an obvious telegraph pole where you have to cross the fairway to a gap in the trees. A rather overgrown path climbs up to a tractor track that runs through some trees, then crosses another fairway with a bell on it and round the edge of a hill to meet a track from the left. This track leads to the Baldernock Primary School and a cottage.

I could see from the map that I had little choice but to follow minor roads all the way from here into Milngavie, but I had no indication it would be such a pleasant route. With the advantage of a bit of height I gazed across rolling countryside, over the skyline of the City of Glasgow towards the distant Gleniffer Braes. The spinning turbines of the mammoth Whitelees windfarm, the biggest in Europe, on the south side of Glasgow, could be clearly seen as was the much more attractive spire of Glasgow University, dwarfed by some of the city's less attractive high-rise flats. Glasgow has had its fair share of bad press throughout the years but few cities have such easy access to rural landscapes like this.

The minor roads took me from the school (marked on the map as Fluchter) and I turned right at the first junction where the winding road led to a T-junction.

The trail north starts from the outskirts of Glasgow at Milngavie and initially follows the start of the popular West Highland Way

I turned right here and then almost immediately left again at Baldernock Parish Church, which dates from 1795. I turned right again at the next road junction and followed a very narrow, dark lane down through the trees, past another golf course, and into the suburb of Milngavie (pronounced Mulguy). This was the end of the road for the second section of the Gore-Tex Scottish National Trail, but also marked the beginning of the third section that would leave the lowlands behind and cross the Highland Line into God's own country.

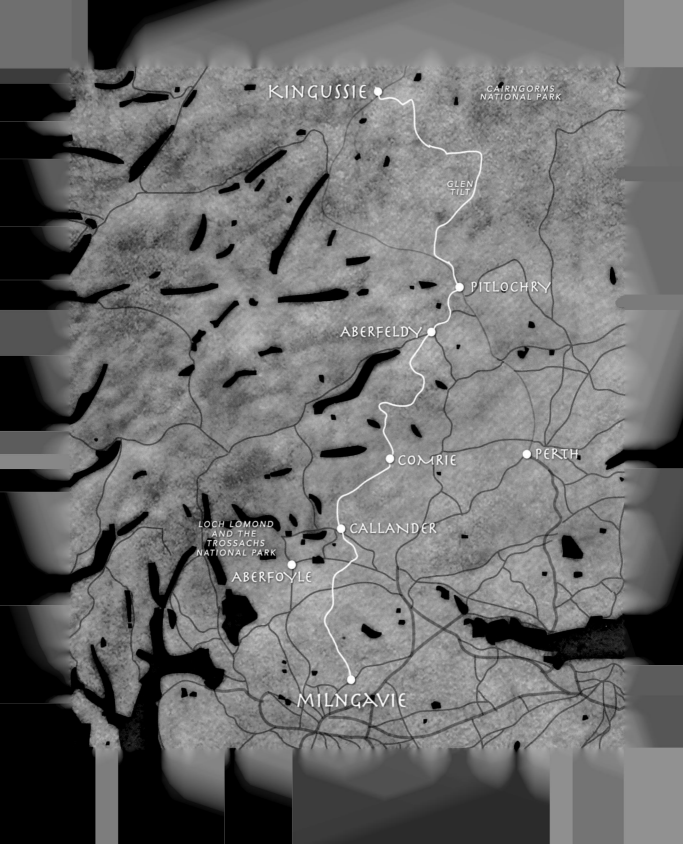

CHAPTER 3

MILNGAVIE TO KINGUSSIE

Start:	Milngavie.
Finish:	Kingussie.
Distance:	200km/125 miles approx.
Public Transport:	See sections below. For more information on public transport in Scotland go to www.travelinescotland.com or phone 0871 200 22 33. Frequent trains from Glasgow to Milngavie. Kingussie has rail and bus links with Glasgow, Perth and Inverness.

General information

For more information on accommodation, visitor attractions etc go to
www.lochlomond-trossachs.org, www.highlandperthshire.org and
www.perthshire.co.uk . You may find Scottish Hill Tracks (published by Scotways)
useful in route checking. Tourist information centres in Aberfoyle, Callander,
Aberfeldy and Pitlochry.

North of Callander with a fine view of Meall Odhar

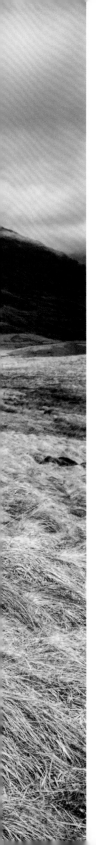

Milngavie to Kingussie

from the Lowlands to the Highlands

For many years, official long-distance trails were a rarity in Scotland. The West Highland Way, Scotland's first official long-distance footpath, has been an enormous success, with thousands of people walking the route between Milngavie, just north of Glasgow, and Fort William every year. The trail brings millions of pounds to the small communities along the way and several dozen full-time jobs have been established because of its existence. Scotland's second oldest route, the Southern Upland Way, with many of its long stretches avoiding villages and towns, has been a little less successful, partly because it was originally designed as more of a 'wilderness' route, avoiding settlements as much as possible. It runs for 340km/212 miles from Portpatrick to Cockburnspath and was Scotland's first coast-to-coast route.

The route of Scotland's third trail, the Speyside Way is, at the time of writing, still awaiting completion. Scottish Natural Heritage and the Cairngorms National Park have been deadlocked with local landowners on a route for the section of the trail that crosses the grounds of Kinrara Estate just outside Aviemore. However, as I write, Scotland's environment minister has just confirmed a compulsory path order (the first in Scotland under the new access legislation) to force Kinrara to allow the Speyside Way across its land. The fourth official trail in Scotland, the Great Glen Way, was opened in 2002 and runs for 128km/79 miles between Inverness and Fort William. There is also a Great Glen canoeing trail, opened in 2012.

As well as being a rarity, official long-distance trails are curious beasts, attracting thousands of walkers who appear reluctant to plan their own routes, averse to the idea of following their own noses instead of signposts and disinclined to leave the beaten track established by others. Perhaps there's a comfort in knowing what the next section of trail will bring, or maybe homo sapiens' herding instinct is still strong in us and like the sheep we're happy to follow in the steps of those who have gone before us. However, the shepherding instinct is obviously alive and well because over the past ten years a host of routes have been designed and signposted all over Scotland to such an extent that Scottish Natural Heritage don't see the need to create any more 'official' routes themselves. They have approved 23 of these new routes and have classified them as *Scotland's Great Trails*, providing over 1,500 miles of well managed paths from the Borders to the Highlands, offering great opportunities to explore the best of Scotland's nature and landscapes and to experience our amazing history and culture. The Gore-Tex Scottish National Trail unashamedly makes use of several of these trails, linking them together with core path networks to form a long and continuous end-to-end route through Scotland.

Not long after the opening of the West Highland Way I'd thought about following it north from Glasgow and linking its northern terminus at Fort William with the ancient Cateran's Road, the Rathad nam Meirleach, to Aviemore, a magnificent traverse of the districts of Lochaber and Badenoch. To complete a wonderful 500km loop that would form a challenging Heart of Scotland Trail, all that remained for me to do was work out a route between Aviemore and Glasgow. I had little idea the remaining side of the triangle would prove to be so different from the other two sections and in its own way turn out to be a walk of superb variety and contrast.

During a ten-day holiday back in the late 1980s I left Milngavie on the West Highland Way and followed it as far as Drymen. I then struck off in a north-easterly direction towards Aberfoyle, Callander, Comrie, Aberfeldy, Blair Atholl, Glen Tilt and over the Lairig Ghru to Aviemore, a long walk that featured some years later in TGO (The Great Outdoors) magazine. I've always had the notion that the walk, which I'd called the Central Highlands Way, could be part of an end-to-end walk from the Borders to the north coast of Scotland and might even provide an alternative to the heavily subscribed West Highland Way.

Loch Venachar – the route north follows beneath Ben Gullipen to Callander

During the planning of the Gore-Tex Scottish National Trail, many people suggested I simply link Glasgow and Fort William by the West Highland Way, a prospect that was rather tempting. The route is a good one, it's well appointed with accommodation and baggage carriers and having walked it several times I knew it intimately, but I felt the West Highland Way was a soft option, an easy way out, and that walking in Scotland could be better served by following another route between the Central Belt and Lochaber/Badenoch. The decision not to use the West Highland Way was confirmed when my wife, an inveterate enthusiast of the route, tried and failed dismally to book accommodation for a trip she had planned during the month of May. I always suspected Scotland's premier backpacking route is overused and my wife's experience underlined that suspicion. I didn't want the Gore-Tex Scottish National Trail to add to that overuse. I went back to my Central Highlands Way idea.

Early morning sun breaks through a group of native silver birch

Milngavie to Aberfoyle

Distance:	38km/24 miles.
Maps:	This section is covered by Ordnance Survey 1:50,000 Landranger sheets 64 and 57.
Public transport:	Frequent trains from Glasgow to Milngavie. Buses from Glasgow to Drymen and Aberfoyle.
Accommodation:	B&Bs in Milngavie. Hotels and B&Bs in Drymen and Aberfoyle.
Route:	Follow West Highland Way signs out of Milngavie and past Drymen to a track junction at 482906. Follow the Rob Roy Way from here to Aberfoyle.

Additional route information

Official guide to the West Highland Way by Roger Smith and Robert Aitken (Mercat Press). The Rob Roy Way by Jacquetta Megarry (Rucksack Readers).

Sharing the first 20km or so with the West Highland Way, the middle link in the Gore-Tex Scottish National Trail follows footpaths, lanes and an old railway line from Milngavie to Drymen before diving into the sprawling Garadhban Forest. After a short distance on forest tracks the West Highland Way crosses the minor public road between Drymen and Gartmore and heads for Conic Hill and Loch Lomond while the Badenoch route parts company here, making its own way towards Gartmore for about 3km to a car park and picnic area near the Drymen Road Cottages from where a trail runs through the Loch Ard Forest to Aberfoyle.

Glengoyne Distillery – reputed to be 'Scotland's most beautiful distillery'

For the next 200km or so, forest tracks, rights of way, footpaths and drovers' roads were to take me on a rough and straggling north-easterly line through forests, along lonely glens, over high passes and across the ridges that form the grain of the Central Highlands.

For parts of the route I followed the signposts on another of Scotland's Great Trails – the Rob Roy Way, a marvellous week-long walk that begins in Drymen and finishes in Pitlochry in highland Perthshire. The route is named after the legendary Scots figure Rob Roy MacGregor Campbell, who probably used many of the same byways himself during a career in which he was, by turn, a hero, a notorious outlaw, a patriot and a successful businessman. The route was the idea of publisher and walking enthusiast Jacquetta Megarry of Rucksack Readers and John Henderson of Walking Support. Jacquetta's popular guide to the route is now in its third edition.

Before I reached the start of the Rob Roy Way in Drymen, I had to get out of Milngavie, a northern suburb of Glasgow. Like the many thousands of walkers who hike the West Highland Way every year I left the shopping centre in the town and followed the WHW signs to Mugdock Country Park. I passed Craigallian Loch where pre-war outdoors folk would congregate around the legendary Craigallian fire, swapping yarns and laying plans, the pioneers of the Scottish outdoor movement that has exploded into the burgeoning numbers who go to the hills today; and on past the wooden huts at Carbeth to Tinker's Loan and the footpath that runs downhill past Arlehaven and Dumgoyach Farm into Strathblane. It's always at this point that I feel I've left the city behind me.

Glasgow is Scotland's largest city, and its tentacles reach far into the countryside that surrounds it, but despite that here, beyond its northern suburbs, you enter a very different landscape. Although you're not technically in the Highlands there is a definite highland feel to it, probably because of the proximity of the great escarpment of the Campsie Fells.

These rolling hills dominate the skyline to the north of Glasgow and are to the city what the Pentlands are to Edinburgh, a high, green horizon which beckons through the urban haze with promises of escape and fresh air. The fells make up a surprisingly large area, from the prominent top of Dumgoyne in the west to the Carronbridge to Kilsyth road in the east. The eastern fells tend to be dominated by forestry plantations but further west, particularly here above Strath Blane, access to the tops is far easier.

As a schoolboy on the south side of Glasgow I used to gaze from my classroom window across the city to the promise of those high hills, desperate for the weekend when I could pack my 'Bergen' and set off from Blanefield, exploring the crags and high moorlands to the accompaniment of whaups, oystercatchers and lapwings. The Campsie Fells have introduced generations of Glaswegians to the delights of hillwalking and mountaineering. As youngsters we would gaze north from the high plateau towards Ben Lomond, the limit of our early ambitions. Beyond the Ben lay another world, as remote to us as the Himalaya or Alaska, a world which we knew very little of, a world well beyond our experience and our imaginings.

The Campsie Fells are made up of layers of lava flow and Dumgoyne, the 'fort of the arrows', the thumb-like addendum that sticks up at the western end of the fells, is an ancient volcanic plug whose name suggests that it was once a defensive site. Curiously, neighbouring Dumfoyne could be 'the hill fort of the wart', which neatly describes its appearance. The area's highest point, Earl's Seat at 578m/1880ft, on the north side of the fells, is probably named after the Earl of Lennox whose lands once extended on the south side of the Campsies. The route of the West Highland Way makes its way round the western extremity of the blunt volcanic plug of Dumgoyne. Below its green slopes the whitewashed buildings of the Glengoyne whisky distillery shone in the sun. Reputed to be Scotland's most beautiful distillery, there has been a distillery here since 1833, producing its excellent lowland single malt but unlike many malt whisky distilleries, Glengoyne doesn't use peat smoke to dry the barley, but instead uses warm air. I wonder if it's that technique that gives the whisky its soft, rounded flavour? It's one of my favourites and I'd certainly recommend it.

I was now following the West Highland Way along the bed of the old Blane Valley Railway, which once carried passengers between Aberfoyle and Kirkintilloch. The Beech Tree Inn stands on the site of the old Dumgoyne Station so I made full use of its facilities and sat outside with my soup and toasted sandwich.

I know this area well – I lived for a while in nearby Fintry when I moved south from the Highlands to take on the job as editor of *Climber* magazine in Glasgow but despite the attractions of the Campsies and the nearby Trossachs, not to mention the fleshpots of the city, my family missed the Highlands badly and after 18 months we moved north again. For the next twenty-odd years while editing first *Climber* and then *TGO* I commuted a couple of days a week between Newtonmore and Glasgow, a one-man contribution to global warming! Not far from the Beech Tree Inn there was once a large hospital with a prominent neuro-surgical unit but it was moved to a new complex in the city leaving the buildings derelict. Beyond the old hospital site, near the ravine known as the Pots of Gartness, stands a house that was once the home of John Napier, the inventor of logarithms. It was said that Napier would often stroll along the banks of the River Endrick at night, clad in his night attire, working on mathematical problems until the cold drove him indoors.

The village square at Drymen where the route follows the Rob Roy Way north

My next stop was the village of Drymen, a very pleasant rural retreat with a shop, a couple of decent hotels and a post office. It may have a rather genteel feel to it today but once upon a time this was the last point of civilisation for the travellers of old before they crossed the Highland Line at the foot of Loch Lomond. The Highland geological fault is a rift between the south of Loch Lomond and Stonehaven on the east coast near Aberdeen, a line that in bygone days struck fear and dread into the hearts of northbound travellers, and understandably so. Once the line was crossed the land became wild and rough, a place where the laws of the land were largely ignored by the inhabitants. Clansmen had their own laws, bowing to no-one but their hereditary chief.

Robbers and vagabonds were a real threat to travellers and many were the outlaws from society who sought sanctuary in the vastness beyond the Highland Line.

This outlaw from society was by now seeking his own sanctuary. The most exhausting thing about walking on the West Highland Way is saying hello to everyone you pass. I guess I could, like some people, just bow my head, look at my feet and ignore all the other walkers, but that always seems rather rude and unfriendly so I tend to give everyone a cheery greeting. The only problem is that over the course of a day the cheeriness evaporates, especially when you become tired and hungry, and the temptation to simply hang your head becomes great. Fortunately I was well aware that once I went beyond Drymen, and the route of the West Highland Way, the numbers of people I met would fall drastically.

For the next 30km I was to follow the line of the Rob Roy Way, first through the Garadhban and Loch Ard Forests to Aberfoyle and then along the line of the rolling Menteith Hills to Callander. All this, and beyond, was once MacGregor territory. The clan's most famous son, Rob Roy MacGregor, was born at Glengyle, on the shores of Loch Katrine, on 7th March 1671, the son of Lt-Col Donald MacGregor, an officer in the army of Charles II, and Margaret Campbell, half-sister to the later despised Campbell of Glenlyon, who was partly responsible for carrying out the orders at the Massacre of Glencoe in 1692. Young Robert grew to be one of Scotland's best-loved characters, though even today there is much disagreement as to whether he was a hero or a villain.

Robert, or as he became widely known, Rob Roy (meaning Red Robert), became chief of the clan on his father's death in 1693. In actual fact he wasn't next in line of descent for the title being only the second son, but such was his personality and influence over his elder brother John, even at the young age of 22, that his brother declined the responsibilities in favour of Rob. History records Rob Roy as not being very tall, but his broad stocky build and strong personal charisma stood him head and shoulders above others in any social gathering. It is said that his mood could change from cold anger to uproarious laughter at the drop of a hat, and he had a devilish sense of humour, greatly enjoying practical jokes and in particular, putting one over on authority!

Cameron on the route accross the Mentieth Hills

He had vowed to help the downtrodden and in those wild days protection like that required a strong show of muscle and arms. He also inherited from his father the Captaincy of the Highland Watch, a type of semi-official blackmail business.

In those days of widespread reiving, bands of men protected the cattle of the rich merchants and farmers who lived on the borders of the Highland Line, in return for an annual fee. In a short time this protection racket became big business, and was even later approved of by the Government, who were no doubt delighted to see the rebel clan chiefs settle down as prosperous businessmen and entrepreneurs! These Watches, as they became known, were set up throughout the Highlands and Rob Roy's father became joint Captain of the Highland Watch. In time, the members of the various Watches took a high social position in the clan set-up – they were in the privileged position of being allowed to carry arms, and they could exercise some authority over their neighbours. This authority was often flouted, and a great amount of cattle stealing, or lifting, went on as well, under the respectable and approved mask of the Highland Watch!

Ben Ledi dominates the skyline west of Callander

Rob Roy ran his Watch in a shrewd business-like manner, and woe betides anyone who was late with his dues, whether he was the local minister, or the Lord Justice Clerk. Rob Roy was no great respecter of rank.

One of the aims of the Gore-Tex Scottish National Trail was to visit both of Scotland's National Parks and later I'd be passing through the Cairngorms Park but for the moment I was walking in the Loch Lomond and Trossachs National Park. Well over a hundred years ago John Muir campaigned for public and political support for his vision that America's finest landscapes should be protected as 'national parks'.

Today, virtually every civilised country in the world boasts its own national park system, although Scotland was relatively late in joining that international fraternity. Before the advent of the Scottish Parliament in Edinburgh National Parks were well down the political agenda of London-based governments but following the establishment of the devolved Holyrood Parliament in 1999, Scottish politicians lost little time in passing legislation for the creation of National Parks in Scotland. John Muir would have greatly approved.

As I've suggested earlier in this book Muir was a wilderness prophet and his writings on the need to cherish wild land and its people, while safeguarding nature, are thought to be even more relevant today than they were in 19th century California where he lived. Some of the aims of the National Parks (Scotland) Act directly relate to Muir's vision, but the added objective of economic development was included by the Scottish Government, presumably to placate local communities, many of whom were highly suspicious of the effects of a National Park designation.

The aims of both parks, as laid out in the Act, include the conservation and enhancement of the natural beauty of the landscape, while promoting sustainability, public enjoyment and social and economic development. More than 14,000 people live within the Loch Lomond and Trossachs Park's 1865 sq km boundaries and as well as familiar landmarks like Loch Lomond and Loch Katrine the Park boasts 21 Munros (mountains over 3000 ft) 33 Corbetts (between 2500 ft and 2999ft), two forest parks and 57 individual sites recognised for their special conservation value. The word 'Trossachs' is derived from *trosaichen*, a word now obsolete in the Gaelic language meaning a transverse glen joining two others, an apt description of the heartland of the area between Loch Katrine and Loch Achray.

Before the 19th century, Loch Lomond and the Trossachs wasn't the tourist haunt it is today. A statistical account of the late 18th century describes it as a land "beyond the border", a district sequestered from the laws of the day and ruled and dictated to by an ancient patriarchal clan system. Travellers were not welcome and foraging parties of clansmen would regularly plunge south on what Sir Walter Scott called "predatory excursions upon their Lowland neighbours". Scott was amongst the first of a number of literary worthies who celebrated the area in song and praised it in prose. The Wordsworths, James Hogg the Ettrick Shepherd, and Robert Burns were among the early tourists.

About a kilometre and a half north of Drymen the routes of the West Highland Way and Rob Roy Way separate, the former to begin the long ascent of Conic Hill overlooking Loch Lomond and the latter to follow a minor road for about 3km to the Old Drymen Road car park where it leaves the minor road and takes to a forest road. Two roads leave the tarmac at this point – the Rob Roy Way follows the right-hand track. During the next few kilometres I couldn't see much for the trees, but I did pass a series of domed shafts, tunnels and aqueducts, all part of the Loch Katrine water scheme. Loch Katrine, as well as being the finest of the Trossachs lochs, is also the main water supply for the City of Glasgow. The loch holds some 14,000 million gallons (over 60,000 million litres) of water at any one time, no doubt due to the average rainfall in the Trossachs of some 85 inches (2125mm) annually.

The quality of the water is extremely high, giving Glasgow the finest supply of any city in the UK. The water supply flows along an underground aqueduct, which is marked above ground by this series of towers and shafts, a 40km journey from Loch Katrine to Glasgow. Work on the aqueduct started in 1855 in typical Victorian fashion – no expense spared. Even today, the aqueducts and ventilation shafts look impressive, and it's obvious from the series of towers which trace the underground route that money was never a problem. Bear in mind that the squads of navvies who built this aqueduct were probably paid no more than subsistence wages. Physical graft came cheap in those days.

My own physical graft was beginning to tell on the final few kilometres into Aberfoyle and I was glad to emerge from the forest at Balleich.

It was only a short walk into the village and my bed and breakfast for the night but before settling down I wanted to visit the ruined Kirkton Church and cemetery. A former church minister here, the Reverend Robert Kirk, was the seventh son of another former Aberfoyle church minister. Kirk was also, for a time, the minister of Balquhidder parish and he was a curious character for he was convinced of the existence of fairies. In 1691 he wrote an amazing book called *The Secret Commonwealth of Elves, Faunes and Fairies* and claimed his knowledge was first-hand!

It's said he was walking one day on Doon Hill, close to the Aberfoyle manse, when he sank to the ground, apparently dead. Shortly after his funeral, he reappeared as a ghost, and explained, "I fell down in a swoon, and was carried into fairyland, where I am now". It was sincerely believed by many of his parishioners that Kirk was indeed a captive of the fairy people, and that his spirit was held within the confines of an old Scots pine tree on the summit of Doon Hill.

The ruined church at Kirkton on the outskirts of Aberfoyle

Less than 50km from the city centre of Glasgow, Aberfoyle sits slap bang on the very edge of the Highlands, on the geological fault line that runs across Scotland from the south end of Loch Lomond to Stonehaven. All before it is lowland. To its north lie the highlands. As such, Aberfoyle has a turbulent history. Graham's *Sketches of Scenery in Perthshire,* published in 1806, explains: "'Tis well known, that in the highlands, it was in former times accounted not only lawful, but honourable, among hostile tribes, to commit depredations on one another; and these habits of the age were perhaps strengthened in this district by the circumstances which have been mentioned. It bordered on a country, the inhabitants of which, while they were richer, were less warlike than they, and widely differenced by language and manners." You won't notice that wide a difference nowadays.

Looking west to Beinn Bhreac on the way north to Comrie

Aberfoyle to Pitlochry

Distance: 76km/48 miles.

Maps: OS Landranger sheets 57, 51, 52 and 43.

Public transport: Buses from Glasgow to Aberfoyle and Callander (via Stirling). Buses from Perth to Comrie and Aberfeldy. Good bus and rail links from Glasgow and Edinburgh to Pitlochry via Perth.

Accommodation: Hotels and B&Bs in Aberfoyle, Callander, Comrie, Aberfeldy and Pitlochry. SYHA hostel in Pitlochry.

Route: Follow the Rob Roy Way from Aberfoyle through the Menteith Hills to Callander. Leave the RRW here and go over Callander Craigs (signposted). At the minor road turn left past Braeleny and continue on the track to Arivurichardich (643138). Take the track heading east into Glen Artney. At Auchinner (694157) take the track on the north side of Glen Artney which eventually becomes a road and leads via Ross Wood into Comrie. Walk up Glen Lednock and at Invergeldie (743277) take the track heading east and then north over the Cam Buidhe bealach (754317) to Dunan. Turn right (east) and walk down Glen Almond to Auchnafree (820335). Turn north into Glen Lochan. At Glenquaich Lodge turn left on a minor road past Loch Freuchie and over a high pass. At a lochan at 801432 turn right (east) on a track that follows the Urlar Burn to the Birks of Aberfeldy, and continue into Aberfeldy. Pick up the Rob Roy Way again and follow it by the River Tay to Grandtully and then over to Pitlochry.

Additional route information

The Rob Roy Way by Jacquetta Megarry (Rucksack Readers). Pitlochry walks leaflet available locally. The section from Callander to Aberfeldy is not on a recognised trail.

The next 18km, over the Highland Edge itself and along the rolling escarpment of the Menteith Hills to the foot of Loch Venachar, certainly emphasised the geographic difference between those districts to the north and to the south of this geological faultline. The southern views take in some of the flattest land in all Scotland – Flanders Moss, leaning eastwards and then opening out towards the distant blue rise of the Ochils, and across to the lowland swell of the Campsie Fells and the Kilpatricks. To the north, a jumble of high hills and mountains dominate, a raised and tumbled land, as different from the south as chalk is from cheese. As I followed the old railway into the town of Callander I passed a field that appeared to be curiously corrugated. This is the site of an old Roman camp, a temporary camp, as the might of the Roman legions never quite managed to quell the Scots to the north of the Antonine Wall. There are also Roman links with Glen Almond further north.

There are a handful of towns in Scotland that boast the nickname 'Gateway to the Highlands' but Callander's claim is more than justified. The town, beautifully situated at the junction of the Teith and Leny rivers, has long been popular as a tourist resort and indeed as a centre for exploring the hills and lochs of the southern Highlands. It's been claimed that Callander has, in proportion to its population, more hotels and guest houses than any other town in Scotland. Despite its popularity with those who want to visit the Highlands, Callander itself is very much a lowland town. It consists of a long, broad main street from which narrower streets and lanes run south towards the River Teith, which forms its southern boundary. The first bridge across the river was built in 1764 and was replaced by the present bridge in 1907. The poet John Keats passed through Callander in 1818, describing it as "vexatiously full of visitors".

The person mainly to blame was Sir Walter Scott, whose novels and writings about the nearby Trossachs, particularly the long romantic poem *The Lady of the Lake*, caught the imagination of the 19th-century public. They flocked to places like Callander and Aberfoyle to experience something of the atmosphere of the Children of the Mist, Rob Roy MacGregor and the Celtic Twilight.

At this point I had decided to part company with the Rob Roy Way for a while. From Callander the Rob Roy Way follows the Sustrans Cycle Route 7 on an old railway track for 15km to Strathyre and then climbs above Lochearnhead and through Glenogle to continue to Killin at the western end of Loch Tay. The route then follows minor roads and tracks along the south shore of Loch Tay to Ardtalnaig and then by way of more minor roads and tracks to Aberfeldy. I wanted to take a more direct line, and try to avoid the hard core cycle track as much as possible by following an old right of way for 25km from Callander to Comrie – by "lone Glen Artney's hazel shade", as Walter Scott put it in his *Lady of the Lake*. According to Stobie's 1783 map of Perthshire the old right of way was once a road.

Behind the town of Callander the beautifully wooded Callander Craigs rise to a height of 340m/1100ft. Early views over Callander towards the distant Gargunnock and Fintry hills were nothing compared to the view that opened up as I reached the summit cairn. I sat in the sun for a good 20 minutes, gazing west along the length of silvery Loch Venachar, its head apparently choked by the high hills of the Trossachs. To the right I could see into the very bosom of Ben Ledi, into its great wild north-eastern corrie, and to the east my gaze carried me along the broad strath to Stirling, the Ochils and beyond to the dim outline of the Pentlands near Edinburgh, which I had crossed on the southern section of the Gore-Tex Scottish National Trail. Beyond the summit cairn, built in 1887 to commemorate Queen Victoria's Golden Jubilee, a footpath descended gently through young birch woods and groves of Scots pine and offered good views over heather moorland, open land that stretched into the long dog-leg of Glen Artney. Here, the gables of a hundred ruins bear testament to former settlements and those who tirelessly worked the land. Today the ubiquitous sheep, the woolly locusts of the Highlands, remind me of what replaced them.

There are remains of Roman camps and standing stones and here and there vitrified forts reflect even older times. The whiffs and taints of antiquity are stronger here than on the West Highland Way, and I was glad I had chosen a different route to make my way north.

Ancient tribes once inhabited these districts between what we now call the Grampians and the River Forth in the south. They spoke not Gaelic, nor Pictish, not even Irish but a form of 'British' that had a relationship to today's Welsh, Cornish or Breton. Known as Verturiones, these ancient people were heavily influenced by the Irish who increasingly occupied the lands, particularly during the Roman occupation. In time the northern area became known as Ath Fhodhla, or New Ireland, nowadays known as Atholl, and further south Strath Eireann, or Ireland's strath, eventually became known as Strathearn. Loch Earn is derived from the same source. Another Irish link is to be found in upper Glen Artney, just north of Callander. Where Gleann a'Chroin rolls down from the great corries of Stuc a'Chroin and Ben Vorlich and meets Glen Artney, a house called Arivurichardich still stands, an old building fully exposed to the winds and the rains that sweep along the length of the open glen. According to the writings of Seton Gordon, the name of the house is a corruption of Airigh Mhuircheartaich, or Moriarty's Shieling, another suggestion of an Irish link in the place-name chain of this vast district.

I camped close to here, drinking in the solitude, revelling in the quietness and beauty of the place. And just as I've experienced a thousand times before, my delight was slightly tarnished by an awareness that people once lived and died here and now, for a whole variety of reasons, such houses as this lie empty and forlorn. I'm always so aware that it's impossible to simply shrug aside the ghosts of yesterday. They are as real as the trumpeting lapwings, the shrieking oystercatchers and the warbling curlews. Often they are as melancholy as the thin piping of the golden plover. You can't ignore the ancient shielings and the dry stone walls, or the gable ends still standing. You can't pretend this kind of wildness is wilderness – unless you are happy to accept that such desolate beauty has been paid for time and time again by the blood of those who came before us, a land redeemed by those who were removed from it.

Meall Odhar on the route between Callander and Comrie

And while you can't deny the sorrow of yesteryear there is no doubt these empty lands now give undeniable joy to many – the landscape's ability to outlive and outshine our attempts, however valiant, at taming it.

From Arivurichardich the track veered east below the slopes of Meall Odhar and Tom Odhar and led me into landscapes that became increasingly open and bare. Nodding its head to the peaks of Beinn Each, Stuc a'Chroin and Ben Vorlich the glen eventually bends away to the north-east before dropping down to its beautiful, wooded lower stretch where the Water of Ruchill cascades down a deep channel towards the village of Comrie. Glen Artney could be from be *Artanag's Glen*, a name based on the old Gaelic word for a bear. For much of its length the glen was an ancient deer forest, supplying venison to the kings and queens of Scotland at Holyrood, Dunfermline and Falkland.

A minor road follows the south banks of the Water of Ruchill all the way from Glenartney Lodge to Comrie but, as keen as ever to avoid the tarmac, I turned left at the black stump of the road and followed a track that led to a bridge over the Allt Srath a' Ghlinne just beyond the farm buildings at Auchinner. From there I followed a rough track for some 13km above the wooded north bank of the river until it eventually morphed into another public road that took me past Ross Wood and the enticingly named Earthquake House and into Comrie. It was wet and windy when I arrived but I was thankful it was nothing worse – small earthquakes are a common occurrence hereabouts. The village is apparently situated close to several geological fault lines and in the 1830s around 7,300 tremors were recorded. Today Comrie remains one of the most geologically active areas in the United Kingdom and records earthquakes more often, and to a higher intensity, than anywhere else in Britain. Consequently, the world's first seismometers were set up here in the 19th century and you can see models of them at the Earthquake House. Perhaps it's not surprising that Comrie is sometimes referred to as the Shaky Toon!

The village lies at the confluence of Glen Artney and Glen Lednock so after a brief lunch in the Comrie Café I set off again, eager to get the 20km or so to Dunan in Glen Almond under my boots. The road up lovely Glen Lednock led eventually to the farm at Invergeldie at the foot of Ben Chonzie and beyond the farm a rough track rose to a bare and windswept bealach that looked down on the remote head of Glen Almond. This is a lonely spot with the sharp spire of the Shee of Ardtalnaig rising abruptly behind the estate building at Dunan. The Corbett of Creagan na Beinne can be climbed from here, by following the broad south ridge easily to the summit, a wide and open wind-scoured place with superb views across the Loch Tay to the Lawers hills. The area of the southern highlands between Loch Tay and Strath Earn is largely made up of rolling hills and high moorlands and while it certainly lacks any distinctive features of a mountainous nature there are several high hills, including the Corbetts of Creag Uchdag (879m/2883ft) and the nearby Creagan na Beinne (888m/2913ft).

Too many times in the past I've avoided great tracts of wild land like this because of a perceived 'dullness', but over the years I've realised that these are the areas where you can find a special blend of solitude, with only the cackle of grouse or the sound of sheep to keep you company. Needless to say, only the most resolute of Corbett-baggers, or long-distance backpackers, tend to forage into the hills to the south-east of Loch Tay. It had been a long day, about 27 kilometres, but it had been fairly easy walking. Next day would be a tad longer as I was keen to get to Aberfeldy and buy some bits and pieces of food. On long walks like this, where I know I'll be passing through various towns and villages en route, I tend to only carry enough food for two or perhaps three days at a time. There's no point in carrying food for days on end when you can buy fresh stuff.

I pitched my tent close to a drystone wall, hoping for some protection from the wind. It had rained on and off all day but the wind had become increasingly strong during the afternoon and I guessed it might be a stormy night. I didn't worry. Once I'm in my tent, inside my goose down sleeping bag and with a brew of hot tea in hand, the weather outside can do what it likes. Looking out through the open doors (I rarely close tent doors, even through the hours of darkness. In this way I can remain connected to the landscape while enjoying the shelter of the tent) I watched the mist roll down the hillside. Later on, as it was becoming dark, a small group of red deer stags slowly munched their way towards me, paying scant attention to my little green tent. I eventually dozed off, relaxed and attuned to the sounds of the wind and the rain pattering on the flysheet.

Beyond Dunan, Gleann a'Chilleine runs in a north-westerly direction, down to Ardtalnaig on Loch Tay, but in the opposite direction a track runs for some 10km down the length of Glen Almond, whose hillsides are largely given over to the farming of sheep and the shooting of grouse. Here and there lie the tell-tale signs of former settlements, not least the memorial cairn built on the site of the Stuck Chapel, a community named after a holy site situated at the head of the burn of the same name. A memorial plaque says: "This cairn is built on the site of the Stuck Chapel in memory of those who gave their lives in the Great War 1914-18". Stuck Chapel comes from the Gaelic, Stuc a'Chaibeil, meaning 'rock (or pinnacle) of the chapel'. Suidhe Ma-Bheathain is shown on Pont's map near the head of Stuck Chapel Burn and this may indicate a dedication of this chapel to Beoan, a saint of British origin who lived before 800AD. The word Suidhe is often used to denote royal, or religious connections.

Looking east down Glen Quaich with Loch Freuchie just visible in the background

I sat for a while below the little waterfall in its clutch of trees and tried to imagine what the place would have been like in former times. There were apparently nine separate buildings here, each stone built with a thatch of heather, bracken or rushes. There would have been cultivation of grain for food and a few animals grazing on the hill and while we generally condemn the highland clearances for the mass removal of people from glens like this there were probably more folk who left voluntarily, frustrated and hungry after poor harvests and potato blights, desperate to start a new life in the colonies. As I sat there, leaning against a gable wall, the solitude was tangible, almost overwhelming, with the mists hanging low over the tops and the winds sighing down the long miles of the glen.

Beyond the farm buildings at Auchnafree the track continues east towards the head of the Sma' Glen, but I turned north and then north-east through the narrow-sided pass of Glen Lochan, which links Glen Almond with Glen Quaich.

There are actually two lochans in the narrow glen – the small Lochan Uaine (the green lochan) and the larger Lochan a'Mhuilinn (the mill lochan), but after a night of rain it was hard to differentiate between lochans and puddles! The wet track eventually squeezed itself out of the glen's confines and ran downhill to Glenquaich Lodge on the shores of Loch Freuchie where a single-track road ran in a rough north-west direction for about 10km to Kenmore at the foot of Loch Tay. Much as I dislike road walking I stuck with the road (not a single vehicle passed me) past Auchnacloich and Garrow to where it began to climb steeply. I stopped for a bit on a prominent zig-zag and enjoyed the views behind me all the way back to Loch Freuchie. I should be honest and admit that what I really enjoyed wasn't so much the view but the clearing weather that was moving in from the south-west. After a couple of days of rain and wind I badly wanted to walk for a while without waterproofs. It looked like I might get my wish.

I followed the hill road as it made its way across the high, rolling plateau, much of it above the 500-metre contour with great views of Schiehallion and the Ben Lawers group, and just before it began to drop down towards Kenmore I turned right at a small lochan and followed a delightful track down the length of the Urlar Burn to the wonderful Birks of Aberfeldy and the wooded glen of the Moness Burn. There are two good times in the year to visit the Birks of Aberfeldy: in the springtime, when the rivers are running high and the waterfalls of the Moness Burn crash and cascade down its rocky bed in dramatic fashion, or in autumn, when the leaves of the trees are changing from green to russet and burnished bronze and the mosses cling to the black, glistening rocks in all shades from yellow to gold. These are the woods that inspired Robert Burns to pen his famous tribute, perhaps not his finest piece of work, but lines that go a long way to reflect the glory of this wooded, rocky chasm.

The braes ascend like lofty wa's,
The foaming stream deep-roaring fa's,
O'erhung wi' fragrant spreading shaws,
The birks of Aberfeldy.

The Bard visited the Den of Moness on 30th August 1787 during his Highland Tour, but now a proposed hydro-electric scheme threatens the very future of this scenic spot. The Birks includes an SSSI and specific objections have been raised about the impact of the proposed scheme on the woodland flora, including the second most important site nationally for the Small Cow Wheat. A moratorium on water abstraction has been agreed between mid-March and mid-May – the 'seeding season' for Small Cow Wheat, but expert botanists are still expressing opposition to the scheme because of its potential impact on the plant. Indeed, the whole environment will potentially be affected by reduction of humidity levels. Most of the time between June to September flow rates over the waterfalls will be reduced to between 27% and 52% of existing flows.

The Moness Den area was planted with deciduous trees in the late 18th century, adding variety to the natural Caledonian pine woodland, which had survived on the steep-sided crags and those parts of the gorge where browsing animals, like sheep and deer, couldn't reach them. But there's a lot more to these woods than just birks, or birch trees. On the lower stretches of the den you'll find beech, rowan, wych elm, hazel and some willow, and higher up the dominant species are oak and the eponymous birch. It's believed that, in places, there has been continuous woodland cover here for around 5,000 years. The more recent tree planting took place in the area in the late 1780s. Much of the gorge is designated as a Site of Special Scientific Interest for its rich plant and animal life. The cool, damp climate is perfect for mosses and it is possible to see at least ten different kinds, in a small area, on the bank near Burns' Seat.

As I wandered down the wooded footpath the scent of wood garlic mixed with the damp, earthy smells of the gorge but at this time of the year the musty atmosphere was even more exaggerated. The variety of habitats provides shelter, nest sites and plenty of ready meals for a host of bird species including warblers, flycatchers and woodpeckers. Pied and grey wagtails wiggled their rumps near the water of the burn, and dippers darted up and down, small, dumpy dark coloured birds with a prominent white bib. I watched them as they submerged into the boiling waters, to walk along streambeds, underwater and against the current, feeding on grubs and insects amongst the stones of the riverbed. Amazing and lovely little birds.

The Birks of Aberfeldy was popularised by Robert Burns and still attracts thousands of visitors today

The developers say that the town of Aberfeldy could benefit to the tune of £10,000-£20,000 a year by the hydro-scheme, but many years ago the area of the Birks was gifted to the whole community of Aberfeldy and there is a strong local feeling that it shouldn't be sold off for £20,000, or less than ten pounds for every resident of the town. At the recent open meeting figures were cited that the Birks produces a benefit to the town of £1.9 million annually through visitor spend.

Evening light on a tiny lochan above Aberfeldy

These figures were open to many significant qualifications, but even if they were only 10% accurate, the economic benefit being risked by the scheme is £190,000. Even if only 10% of these visitors were lost because of reduced waterfalls the loss would be £19,000 – well above suggested lease rental income – at a time when the town needs every visitor it can get to help sustain local businesses and employment. I'm assured the community of Aberfeldy is in favour of the environmental production of electricity – this area is home to many hydro schemes, from small burns to the massive schemes in the Ben Lawers area, but the area will soon see (literally) the Griffin Forest wind farm and the new huge pylons for the Beauly-Denny power line. Surely the Aberfeldy area has done its bit – the Birks should not be added to this list.

It felt good to be back in the highland Perthshire town. The settlement here began to grow when General Wade built his bridge across the River Tay in 1733 and it has never looked back. It lies on the intersection of two busy roads, the A826 to Crieff and the A827 which leads east towards the A9 Perth to Inverness trunk road. During my former Central Highland Way walk I followed a combination of rough paths and a quiet road along the northern banks of the River Tay to Edradynate where a minor road climbed high above the meandering river past the farms of Blackhill and Lurgan. Another hill track then took me over the Farragons, past Loch Derculich and the rugged eastern slopes of Farragon Hill itself before turning north-east to pass close to the summit of Beinn Eagagach at well over 600 metres. A long and winding descent led to Loch Tummel where further progress northwards was suddenly halted by the broad expanse of water, and the fast flowing River Tummel. I had little inclination to swim across the loch, even without the heavy pack that hung from my shoulders, but could its outflow river be crossed, enabling me to continue over the hill to Blair Atholl? I wanted to keep a north-bound momentum and not have to deviate too far east, or God forbid, too far south, and I desperately wanted to avoid public roads as much as possible.

In 1902 it was recorded in the *Bathymetrical Survey of the Fresh-water Lochs of Scotland* that Loch Tummel was 2.75 miles (4.5km) in length with a maximum breadth of half a mile (800m). Subsequently, a dam was built at the eastern end of the loch, raising its level by some 17 feet (5m) and flooding new areas. As a result the loch is now closer to 11km long and has more than doubled its breadth. But the dam that caused the swelling of the loch and flooded any possible crossing points ultimately proved to be my salvation. Despite the prominent *No Access* signs I sneaked across the dam walkway which spans the new outflow of the loch, mentally preparing a snivelling excuse should I be stopped by some zealous hydro-board official, to reach the north shore and my route to Glen Fincastle and beyond. From the top of the glen the rising road pointed directly over the hill to Blair Atholl and the Cairngorms. After the uncertainty of crossing Strath Tummel, the long miles of Glen Tilt and the stony climb over the Lairig Ghru were a piece of cake.

The route of the Gore-Tex Scottish National Trail was a different kettle of fish though. I couldn't be seen to encourage people to ignore *No Access* signs. That simply wouldn't do, but fortunately in 2008 a 7km section of riverside pathway was created between Aberfeldy and Grandtully, a section that has been adopted by the Rob Roy Way as a means of avoiding a long road walk. From Grandtully I planned to stick with the Rob Roy Way over Dunfallandy Hill and down to the busy town of Pitlochry. This is the endpoint of the Rob Roy Way, but I planned to make use of the town's excellent network of riverside paths to take me through the Pass of Killiecrankie, where a quiet minor road runs for about 4km into Blair Atholl and the southern entrance to the Cairngorms National Park.

After an excellent B&B in Aberfeldy and a shopping session in the supermarket I followed the A827 out of the town, past Dewar's World of Whisky and the cemetery (I don't think the two are intentionally connected) and onto the new riverside walk along the banks of the Tay. It was a lovely start to the day. The river flowed in stately fashion, gathering itself for the downstream rapids at Grandtully, an area that has become very popular amongst white water rafters and kayakers. Incidentally, my hostess in the B&B in Aberfeldy corrected me on the proper pronunciation of Grandtully – it should be spoken as *grant-ly*. For some curious reason the Ordnance Survey has insisted in printing the name as Grandtully, inserting a 'd' where there wasn't one before. This has led to the common pronunciation as *grand-tully*. It's a popular spot with river enthusiasts and boasts an excellent hostel, with its own CAMRA award-winning bar!

From Grandtully I crossed the metal bridge over the Tay, turned right at a War Memorial and followed the road along the edge of a golf course. It wasn't long before I came across a reassuring sign – Public Footpath to Pitlochry! I've always been a strong and enthusiastic advocate of good navigation. Being able to use a map and compass properly is, as far as I'm concerned, the most important skill a walker can learn. Indeed, I would say it's a vital skill. But on a long walk like this the reassurance that often comes from a simple signpost can be wonderful, especially when you are walking through semi-urban areas where an ordinary 1:25,000 scale map doesn't always show all the information you need.

A memorial commemorating the Black Watch lies alongside the river in Aberfeldy

Beyond the sign the footpath was fairly evident on the ground – into the golf course, along a path between dry-stone walls, onto open sheep grazing land and uphill to a kissing gate. Open moorland then led to the entrance to the Fonab Forest where forest tracks led past the remains of the Clachan an Diridh stone circle, thought to be at least 3,600 years old, and down to the busy A9. After the peace of the forest descent it was a shock to stand and watch buses, cars and articulated lorries thunder past me. It actually took me a few moments to mentally prepare myself to cross the road.

Early morning light over the hills of Drumochter

118   *Milngavie to Kingussie*

Pitlochry to Kingussie

Distance:	86km/53 miles.
Ascent:	920m/3400ft approx.
Maps:	OS Landranger sheets 43 and 35.
Public transport:	Good bus and rail links from Glasgow and Edinburgh to Pitlochry and Kingussie.
Accommodation:	Hotels and B&Bs in Pitlochry, Blair Atholl and Kingussie. SYHA hostel in Pitlochry, private hostel in Kingussie. No accommodation on the route itself after Blair Atholl.
Route:	From Pitlochry follow the waymarked path by Loch Faskally and the River Garry to the NTS Visitor Centre at Killiecrankie. Follow minor road into Blair Atholl. Follow track and path up Glen Tilt and over the watershed. Cross the Geldie Burn at 005868 (no bridge), turn left (west) and follow the path by the Geldie to the head of Glen Feshie. Follow the tracks down Glen Feshie past Ruigh-aiteachan bothy, cross the river at 850965 then go via Stronetoper, Corarnstilmore and Baileguish to Drumguish and Tromie Bridge. Follow the Badenoch Way to Ruthven Barracks and the minor road into Kingussie.

Additional route information

Apart from the short section on the Badenoch Way at the end, this section is not part of a recognised trail route.

Dating from 1733, General Wade's iconic bridge crosses the River Tay at Aberfeldy. When it was built there was no modern day town

Safely on the other side of the A9, I passed the Pitlochry Festival Theatre and crossed a narrow pedestrian suspension bridge into the town. The few moments I had taken to prepare myself to face crossing the A9 were well spent – entering Pitlochry was almost as much of a shock. There were people everywhere, tour buses disgorged their passengers in the car park, cars crawled along the busy high street and, after having to queue for 20 minutes for a bar lunch I made a rapid exit. I am well aware of the importance of tourism, but honeypots like Pitlochry can sometimes be too much for a peace-loving soul like me. It reminded me of the old man on Skye who once suggested that tourists would be better to stay at home and just send their money…

I made my way to the car park nearest the dam where there is a visitor centre explaining how hydro-electric power works, and a fish ladder, created to provide safe passage for salmon and trout returning upriver to spawn. A signposted path led me along the east shore of Loch Faskally. This, despite its appearance, isn't a natural loch, having been created as part of a large hydro-electric scheme about 40 years ago. The surrounding area is well wooded with fine deciduous plantations – a joy to witness in autumn and into early winter. I continued past the grounds of Faskally House, a mansion until recently used as an outdoor centre by Strathclyde Region and before long I found myself walking alongside the Garry, one of two fine rivers feeding Loch Faskally. I passed under the high bridge that carried the B8019 road and followed a fine riverside path all the way to Killiecrankie. The Pass itself is pretty awesome. Not only does it carry the A9 trunk road, but it also squeezes in a minor road, a railway line, the footpath I was following, and a tumultuous river.

At a prominent bend in the River Garry, the National Trust for Scotland visitor centre celebrates the Battle of Killiecrankie. In July 1689 this was the scene of a famous victory for the Jacobite forces under the leadership of John Graham of Claverhouse, better known as Bonnie Dundee, who was unfortunately killed in the battle. A soldier called Macbean is said to have escaped by making a spectacular jump across the River Garry at the spot now known as Soldier's Leap. I much preferred the idea of crossing the river by the bridge beyond the Visitor Centre, but there again, I didn't have a dragoon of redcoats chasing me... Once over the river I followed a minor road along the south bank of the Garry to Strathgarry, where it went under the viaduct of the A9 and led to a footbridge over the River Garry and into the heart of Blair Atholl and Scotland's second National Park. It was only recently that the Cairngorms National Park was extended to include the wild and remote Atholl Deer Forest and the communities of Blair, Calvine and Bruar. When the formation of the Park was first announced the southern entrance was in Drumochter Pass. It was felt that certain councillors and politicians were keen to keep control of the park in Highland Council so Highland Perthshire was snubbed.

This controversy, plus the announcement that the official opening of the National Park would take place at the top station of the equally controversial funicular train on Cairn Gorm, encouraged a number of MSPs from all political parties, local councillors from North Perthshire, and various members of organisations who objected to the location of the opening jolly to hold an 'alternative' opening on the summit of Carn Liath, part of the Beinn y Ghlo massif, those marvellous hills that rise to the east of Killiecrankie, the natural, logical and sensible gateway to the Cairngorms National Park.

I found it rather sad that the funicular was chosen for what should have been a very important occasion. I felt the controversial location would forever link Scotland's newest National Park with what is considered by many to be £14.8 million of unsustainable rural development. The metaphor appeared to be very clear – Scottish National Parks are obviously to be a curious mix of nature conservation and commercial development, unlikely bedfellows at the best of times, a mix that will doubtless ensure the Cairngorms' ongoing conservation war of attrition. Almost every other National Park in the world has nature and landscape conservation as its prime objectives. Indeed, many have nature conservation as their only objective, but the die was cast early in the legislative process that led to the National Parks (Scotland) Act when MSPs and Ministers decided economic development was to be one of the prime objectives of Scottish national parks. Such a decision, designed to placate opponents of the National Park concept, simply ensured a future of ongoing controversy. Sadly, the new authority hasn't helped matters by not only giving two fingers to all those who passionately believe we shouldn't have trains running up our major mountains, but by alienating two major landowners. The RSPB and the National Trust for Scotland both fought against the funicular proposals, and now the Park board expects them to come tamely to heel at their bidding.

What a pity the board didn't choose Mar Lodge for the official opening of the Park or almost anywhere in Rothiemurchus, wonderful settings in the richness of the varied landscape that has made the Cairngorms such a unique area. Instead the board chose to continue down the path of controversy – no doubt encouraged by

In the course of its 470 miles, the Trail passes through a tremendous variety of landscape – these are silver birches in the lower reaches of Glen Tilt

those Highland politicians who were determined to keep the focus of the National Park well within their own patch. Thankfully the Scottish National Party, when they became the government of Scotland, changed the boundaries of the National Park at the first opportunity and Blair Atholl and the wonderfully wild land of the Atholl Deer Forest are now part of the UK's largest National Park. I pitched my tent on the campsite and wandered off to the post office to collect a parcel of food that I had previously sent there to be collected. The lady in the shop was keen to hear about my walk – she recognised me from the telly!

With a couple of days food packed away my rucksack felt slightly heavier in the morning as I made my way to Old Blair, the Old Bridge of Tilt and the track that runs up Glen Tilt. I passed the firing range (when red flags are flying avoid it for fear of getting accidentally shot) and dropped down to Gilbert's Bridge, named after Gilbert Stewart, one of the last of the Atholl men to have 'been out' with the Jacobites at Culloden. From the arched stone structure I gazed down on angry waters; brown and rollicking, peat-stained and tumultuous, frothed and bubbling – the cataract of a thousand hill burns (not to mention the Rivers Tarf and Fealar) gathered together and compressed into the confines of the Tilt gorge, seething downhill on its rocky course to join the River Garry some 5km downstream. In an aquatic sense it was as coldly impressive as watching an avalanche roar down a mountainside.

Beyond Gilbert's Bridge the track winds its way up the length of Glen Tilt, past Forest Lodge and eventually across the high watershed into Glen Geldie and Deeside, one of the great through-routes of Scotland, an ancient right of way that was once challenged by the Duke of Atholl. The attempt of the 6th Duke (1814-1864) to close the glen to the public was successfully contested by the Scottish Rights of Way Society who, after a long and lengthy legal debate, established their credentials as Scotland's leading authority on rights of way issues. No problems with access today, of course, and the Atholl Estate has embraced the concept of responsible freedom to roam. Indeed, it's been smarter than that and 'manages' access through a system of signed footpaths that have become very popular with the visiting public.

The great Scots mountain writer W.H. Murray once suggested that Glen Tilt is a place where walkers will never find their interest flagging – the river is always lively, the woods are mature and varied and there is a continuous, gradual change from its lower fertility to an upper desolation where oystercatchers and lapwings provide the summer music. He was right. The sun shone warmly as I made my way north and I was sorely tempted, time and time again, to simply sit by the banks of the river and gaze up at the high slopes of Beinn y Ghlo in front of me, watching the deer, listening to the cackle of grouse and the melodious song of the skylark and just enjoying the physical and mental relaxation of being at peace with the world in such magnificent surroundings.

Wherever possible our new National Trail makes use of existing routes – this is the right of way through Glen Tilt

There was a growing awareness as I tramped the empty miles of a gradual constriction as the valley narrowed to a cleft, a defile, before broadening out again to a windswept and wild beauty. The ruins of the old Bynack shieling remain here, a soft spot in the harshness of these high moors, a place where I've camped many a time before. Beyond the ruins I was aware I was reaching a watershed, a divide. To the west lay the empty miles of Glen Geldie, reaching out to its own watershed with upper Glen Feshie, as wild and remote a spot as you're likely to find in these islands. To the north lay Glen Dee and the nascent River Dee, just beginning to mature into adolescence and growing rather lively after its birth pangs high on the plateau above the An Garbh Coire of Braeriach, Britain's third highest mountain. The river partly followed the route of the Lairig Ghru, the best known of all Scotland's high passes, cutting its way through the Cairngorms like a knife through butter.

An early spring morning in Glen Feshie

My natural instinct had been to include the Lairig Ghru in the route of the Gore-Tex Scottish National Trail, but an avalanche of advice, most of it well considered, convinced me not to tempt the unwary backpacker into a traverse of the Lairig. The summit of the pass reaches a height of 835m/2755ft and it can hold snow well into the summer. It's a curious thing but despite having written extensively about Scotland's Munros and Corbetts I've never had anyone accuse me of tempting the unwary on to our highest mountains, but the Lairig Ghru obviously casts a different level of concern. A few years ago a well known British outdoor magazine aroused a storm of protest when one of its authors suggested the Lairig was one of the places hillwalkers could go in winter without having to bother about crampons and ice axes. The suggestion was that it never snowed in the Lairig Ghru.

How such a suggestion made it to print in a magazine that claims to be the UK's top-selling hillwalking magazine beats me. Thirty years ago there was an attempt to create a Central Highlands Way but members of the Cairngorm Mountain Rescue Team scuppered the plans with their concerns that inexperienced people would be tempted to cross the pass in all weathers. Elements of those concerns still exist, enough to make me abandon plans to take the National Trail over the pass to Rothiemurchus and Aviemore and instead turn west at the head of the Tilt and climb over the lower, but even more remote watershed between Glen Geldie and one of the most beautiful glens you will find in this country of beautiful glens, Glen Feshie. Care is needed for this route as the Geldie Burn can rise very quickly after heavy rain and can be very difficult to cross.

Glen Geldie is a wonderfully wild and open place, and every so often some well-meaning councillor or politician comes up with the idea of having a road run through it, connecting with Glen Feshie to create a motorable route between Deeside and Speyside. In the 1720s General Wade surveyed a potential line, as did the engineers Telford and Mitchell in 1828. Even in relatively modern times the idea, like a bad penny, is aired from time to time. I would stick my neck out and say it will never happen – the cost is far too prohibitive nowadays and both glens lie within the Cairngorms National Park. I can't see any Park board, no matter how pro-development they may be, allowing a project like that to occur. Glen Geldie can be bleak, and the monoculture of the deer estates leaves the hillsides barren and devoid of trees – a wet desert! The stretch of narrow footpath to the watershed with Glen Feshie can be frustratingly slow but the tumultuous flow of the River Eidart breaks the monotony as it crashes downhill from its birthplace high in Coire Mharconaich of the Moine Mhor. A solid iron bridge carries you across the deep chasm to where the footpath drops down to a green sward by the River Feshie and the remains of several shielings. From here the footpath follows the river closely until it meets the pine trees of upper Glen Feshie.

Take visitors into most mountain areas of the Scottish highlands and they will most probably gasp in wonder at the natural beauty that lies before them.

The size and shape of the hills, the sheer expanse of sky and the humbling awareness of human insignificance is not unusual but in many cases those visitors will be looking at a land that is degraded, shorn of its indigenous vegetation, bare of trees, and lacking in biodiversity. Caledonia stern and wild but not entirely natural. It's well known that pine and birch woods once covered much of our uplands but less than one percent of this natural woodland remains. Man's not entirely to blame – a wetter climate and peat formation have played their part as have burning, deliberate forest clearance and overgrazing.

In recent years serious attempts have been made to encourage the regeneration of the remnants of the Caledonian Pine Forest that once covered much of the highlands. In Glen Affric, Rothiemurchus, Glen Tanar and Abernethy, to name a few, there is evidence of new growth as young pines, birches, rowans and aspen are given the opportunity to flourish. At the foot of Coire Ardair on Creag Meagaidh, near Laggan, a birch wood that was dying was brought back to life in all its biodiversity, by simply removing the browsing animals that fed off any young seedlings that dared to poke their heads through the earth. And now Glen Feshie estate, once described as the "jewel in the crown of the Cairngorms" has put the regeneration of the pine forest at the top of its management plans.

Glen Feshie will always be associated with the 19th century artist Sir Edwin Landseer and his painting, *Monarch of the Glen*. That iconic red deer stag has become a symbol to those who oppose the estate's plans to regenerate the woods by culling large numbers of deer. The latest owner of the estate, Danish clothing millionaire Anders Holch Povlsen, wants to more than double the area of native woodland from the existing 1,900 hectares and he plans to do that by maintaining the number of deer at a lower density than previously. Under Feshie Estate's previous ownership, a large cull of red deer had taken place in partnership with the Red Deer Commission, a cull that led to allegations of "wildlife crime" by the Scottish Gamekeepers Association. More recently there has been criticism of the estate's plans from community leaders in nearby Kincraig, who claim that the proposed regeneration will turn the estate into a woodland "jungle". But after only a few years of this regeneration management, the changes to the face of the landscape are marked and positive.

It is wild, remote countryside between between Glen Tilt and the Geldie Burn

Young pines are growing on the roadside slopes, young birch trees are abundant and there is a freshness and a vibrancy in the glen that suggests nothing less than complete renewal. Capercaillie have been seen in the glen again and blackcock numbers are rising. Red deer still roam the woodlands and the slopes around the Glen – there are just fewer of them now.

Glen Feshie wears its "jewel" description with some justification. The area has a long history of people living and working here, and during the 18th and 19th centuries large quantities of pine timber were taken from the woods in the glen. This extraction continued before and during the first and second world wars.

The ruins of Bynack Lodge are a distinctive landmark just south of the Geldie Burn

Feshie was greatly favoured by Queen Victoria and the natural beauty and mystery of the glen inspired Edwin Landseer. Such inspiration is not surprising – there is a sense of timelessness at work here. It's an intriguing thought that some of the older trees, the so-called 'granny' pines, are between 250 and 300 years old, so 30 generations of these trees take us back to the end of the last ice age! These gnarled and knotted old trees are rock hard and anchored deep. Their orange-red trunks contrast vividly with their bottle-green foliage and you can feel their antiquity in the rough bark. And nature has woven an immaculate carpet of lichens and mosses on the woodland floor – juniper and heather live alongside bilberry and cowberry, and wintergreen chickweed and orchids open in the sunlight of summer.

It's a beautiful environment, but it has, until recently, been shrouded in the hush of an old folks' home. There has been no progeny, no youngsters coming through, because the deer have been eating them.

Go there now on a bright spring morning and you'll find the place glistening with new growth and alive with birds – crested tit, tree pipit, dipper, common sandpiper, skylark, wryneck, jay and crossbill in or near the woodlands and golden eagle, peregrine, dotterel, ptarmigan, red and black grouse, dunlin, greenshank and ring ouzel on the hills and moorlands. In addition to red and roe deer the mammals include mountain hare, brown hare, otter, badger, fox, wildcat, pine marten, weasel, stoat, water vole, red squirrel and moles. Pine martens are resident and wildcats have been seen in the lower glen.

Two years ago my wife and I had been mountain biking in Glen Feshie and as we trundled down the estate road I became aware of a large Range Rover drawing alongside us. I'm afraid my pre-Land Reform Act bogies are still alive, and my natural instinct was to expect some form of confrontation about access, but I was wrong. A young tousle-haired man leapt out, introduced himself as Thomas MacDonell, the estate factor, and asked if we had noticed the regeneration in the glen! His bubbling enthusiasm was infectious. We had, in fact, been delighted and amazed to see the abundance of new growth in the glen – pines, juniper, rowan, birch – the glen was being transformed, and much of that transformation can be put down to the vision and enthusiasm of Thomas MacDonell himself.

Born and bred in nearby Kincraig, Thomas has known this estate all his life and witnessed at first hand the problems created by too many deer. It was while working as a fencing contractor, building fences around little tracts of woodland for the Nature Conservancy Council and then Scottish Natural Heritage that he came across deer that were starving to death. During the harsh winter months in particular, there simply wasn't enough food to feed the high numbers of deer that existed. Secondly, he realised that the vegetation within the fenced enclosures grew in unsightly blocks that looked unnatural. The fences themselves looked out of place in such wild landscapes and posed a threat to birds, particularly capercaillie. Surely, he thought, there must a management solution whereby deer occupancy could exist with the emergence and growth of seedlings?

The view north to the Cairngorm mountains from above the Geldie Burn

The answer, of course, was to reduce the number of deer to a level that was compatible with seedling growth, and, armed with this realisation, Thomas set out to discover as much as he could about the balance between deer management and conservation. Red deer management is an extremely complex subject but the challenge to land managers is simple enough – how to get the right deer numbers to maintain benefits to people in jobs, in venison and in tourism against the potential damage to wildlife habitats. Red deer have also become a problem on Scotland's roads, particularly in winter when they are attracted by the salt put down by road gritters.

Thomas MacDonell's family have long been entrenched in farming and sporting estate activity, so he was well aware of the controversies that surround deer management, particularly the anxiety that existed in sporting estates to keep deer numbers high. He decided to work with a range of people to learn and promote understanding about the need to manage deer in a way that takes into account a wide range of interests and perspectives. Those interests include commercial deer stalking, tourism and nature conservation. He quickly learned that management is about getting the correct deer density, or the number of deer divided by the area of land, so the impacts they cause are acceptable to all who use the land. When Glen Feshie was sold to Anders Holch Povlsen in 2006, Thomas lost little time in sharing his vision with his new boss. The Dane was receptive, and immediately began plans to further expand and improve low-level woodlands while also restoring mountain woodlands with rarer species such as aspen, holly and oak. He has already spent a considerable amount of money in repairing and maintaining footpaths, and the old electricity poles that once marched up the glen have been removed and the cables put underground. Over the next five years, the estate hope to more than double the area of native woodland from the existing 1,900 hectares to around 4,000 hectares. Some planting will be carried out in areas where the seed source is missing but most of the increase will come from natural regeneration.

"We want to do it in a way that will improve the quality of this wonderful and special place, while maintaining local employment", Thomas told me. "Indeed, in years to come when the deer settle in the forest again it won't be so easy to cull them. It'll be a cat and mouse game trying to shoot them in the trees. That's when we'll need to employ more stalkers – there are definitely employment opportunities in conservation. I reckon that in the next few years we'll have to shoot about 400 deer every year to maintain a deer density that's compatible with the regeneration of the woodlands, and that's without building any fences. That's not an unusually high figure, other estates about the same size as Glen Feshie will have culling targets that are very similar." Regenerating woodland along the riverbanks will help freshwater life including the Atlantic salmon, and both Thomas MacDonell and Anders Holch Povlsen are keen to further expand and improve low-level woodlands while also restoring mountain woodlands with rarer species.

The deserted cottage at the head of the Geldie Burn which leads west and north to Glen Feshie

I asked Thomas to paint a picture of how he would like to see the estate in the future.

"I want to see a much larger network of woodlands on the estate, a return to how it would have looked during the heyday of the Great Pine Forest of Caledon", he enthused. "I want to see more trees growing in the deeper soils and shelter of the low ground. The forest should be patchy and varied in nature, with lots of clearings and open spaces. Higher up there should be a low-growing cover of gnarled and twisted undersized trees, made up of pine, birch, willow and juniper, trees that are capable of coping with the exposure and thinner soils. And on the mountain tops, dwarf trees like the mountain willow should be clinging to the land, surviving the harsh conditions by nestling among the carpet of mountain mosses and sedges."

Already the glen is beginning to take on that varied and natural cloak and I thoroughly enjoyed wandering below the gnarled and ancient pines, past the ruins and the bothy at Ruigh-aiteachain, and down the east bank of the river to the footbridge just before the farm at Achlean. A major bridge further upstream, at Carnachuin, was swept away in a storm a few years ago and, because of various bureaucratic planning difficulties, has not yet been replaced.

Now on the west bank of the Feshie, I followed the tarmac estate road past the house at Stronetoper and entered the gloomy shade of commercial forestry. Not far beyond the house a forest track ran off to the left and I followed it, leaving the forest behind again just before the fields of the abandoned Corarnstilmore farm. A footbridge crosses the Allt Fhearnasdail, a tributary of the Feshie, where another forest track crosses a high ridge of ground and drops down to the hamlet of Drumguish. Kingussie was now only 5km away.

Rather than walk along the road into Kingussie I followed the route of the Badenoch Way from the single-arched Tromie Bridge towards the 18th century ruins of Ruthven Barracks. The Way is suitable for all the family and it runs for almost 18km between Dalraddy, on the old A9 near Aviemore, to the RSPB Reserve at Ruthven, just outside Kingussie. The route follows a series of paths and tracks over moors, alongside lochs, through forests and woodland and along riverbanks to finish in the gaunt shadow of the Ruthven Barracks.

I've walked the route several times, and parts of it countless times. My family spent four very happy years living in Kincraig, midway along the route, and the section from Speybank to Kincraig became as familiar as the lines on my hand. Many a day I sat beneath an ancient oak and gazed through my binoculars at ospreys hunting by the gravels on the confluence of the Feshie and the Spey. On days of rapid snowmelt in the mountains I've watched the Feshie roar into the confluence with such force that the waters of the Spey were backed up beyond Loch Insh causing the Insh Meadows to flood. The power of nature can be a terrible, and thrilling thing to behold!

The last section into Kingussie was delightful, even though I was back on tarmac. Watching oystercatchers and lapwings cleave their tremulous course and curlews and redshank offering their unique melodies from the waterlogged expanse of the Insh Meadows took my mind off the effect of a hard road and there, sitting on the edge of the marshes, lay Ruthven Barracks, destroyed by clansmen fleeing from Culloden in 1746. It was only a short walk into Kingussie from here, where there are shops, cafés and a bunkhouse. The town also marked the end of the third section of the Gore-Tex Scottish National Trail. The next section, from Kingussie to Cape Wrath, was to be the toughest, remotest and most wonderful of them all.

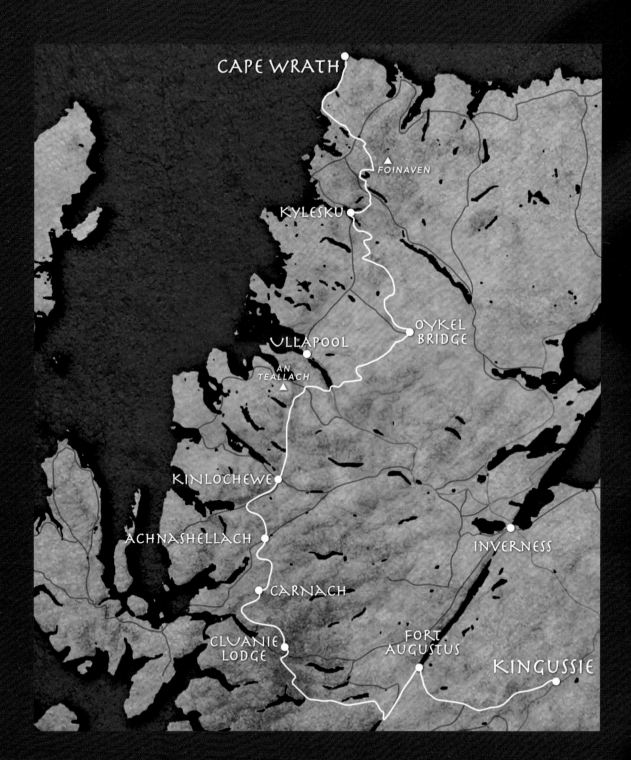

CHAPTER 4

KINGUSSIE TO CAPE WRATH

Start: Kingussie

Finish: Cape Wrath

Distance: 354m/220miles approx.

Public Transport: See sections below. For more information on public transport in
                      Scotland go to www.travelinescotland.com or phone 0871 200 22 33.

General information

For more information on accommodation, visitor attractions etc visitcairngorms.com.
www.kingussie.co.uk, www.newtonmore.com, www.fortaugustus.net, www.lochalsh.co.uk,
www.visittorridon.co.uk, www.ullapool.com, www.oykelbridge.com, www.durness.com

To return from Cape Wrath you will need to take the minibus (01971 511284, 07742 670
196, james.mather5038@btinternet.com) that runs between the Ozone Café at Cape Wrath
and the ferry (01971 511246) that will take you across the Kyle of Durness to Keoldale.
From there it's a 3km walk into Durness, or follow the coastal path from Keoldale to
Balnakeil. Durness lies just beyond Balnakeil. The bus and ferry run every day between
May and September. Outside the main season you will have to walk back to Sandwood Bay
and Kinlochbervie for ongoing public transport. A regular bus runs from Durness to
Kinlochbervie then on to Lairg to meet the Inverness train. It leaves Durness at 8:10am.

The moon sets over a deserted, wintry, Glen Banchor west of Newtonmore

Kingussie to Cape Wrath

Central Highlands to the magical North West

L ying on the edge of the rolling Monadhliath Mountains, the village of Kingussie is well known among outdoor folk. At one time there were more qualified mountain guides living there, per head of population, than in Chamonix in the French Alps and the proximity of the Cairngorms has attracted a legion of enthusiastic hillwalkers, climbers and mountain bikers to the area. Even more noteworthy, the town's shinty team is, according to the Guinness Book of Records, the most successful sporting team in the world having won 20 consecutive league titles and at one point, in the early 1990s, gone four years without defeat. That's very impressive.

This notable achievement is much to the chagrin of neighbouring Newtonmore. Only five kilometres physically separate the two communities, but emotionally they are divided by a hundred years of shinty rivalry. Even today there are individuals who refuse to attend events in either villages and I clearly recall helping organise a folk club in Newtonmore in the 1980s when folk music enthusiasts from Kingussie wouldn't join because it was being held in "the opposing camp". Curiously, it was the creation of a Sustrans cycle-track between the two villages that began to break down the barriers. People now walk between Kingussie and Newtonmore and perhaps do a little shopping; young mothers push their prams along the track and have morning coffee in either village and the old rivalry is becoming less intense. Less intense, that is, until either team wins a title like the Camanachd Cup, the MacTavish Cup or the Marine Harvest League and suddenly the old rivalries flare up again.

A winter morning's view to the Monadhliadh

Kingussie to Achnashellach

Distance:	7 days/168km/105mls: Kingussie to Melgarve: 32km/20mls; Melgarve to Fort Augustus: 20km/12 miles; Fort Augustus to Tomdoun: 28km/18mls; Tomdoun to Cluanie: 20km/12mls; Cluanie to Morvich: 23km/14mls; Morvich to Killilan in Glen Elchaig: 20km/12mls: Glen Elchaig to Achnashellach Station: 25km/15mls.
Maps:	This section is covered by Ordnance Survey Landranger 1:50,000 sheets 41, 34, 33 and 25
Public transport:	For Start and Finish: Kingussie is well served by bus and rail links to Glasgow, Edinburgh and Inverness. Achnashellach is on the Inverness to Kyle of Lochalsh rail line and is also served by bus links from Inverness. Traveline: 0871 200 2233, www.travelinescotland.com. Scotrail, 08457 48 49 50, wwwscotrail.co.uk
Accommodation:	Hotel and hostel at Laggan Bridge; wide choice in Fort Augustus; Forest Lodge Guest House, South Laggan; the Tomdoun Lodge Hotel: 01809 511218 has a growing reputation as a good staging post for backpackers; the Cluanie Inn is a traditional climbers and walkers hostelry and it's not too far from Morvich down to the Kintail Lodge Hotel. Killilan in Glen Elchaig might prove difficult but Gerry's Hostel at Craig, near Achnashellach (01520 766232) is well known amongst the Scottish outdoors cognescenti.
Route:	From Kingussie follow the new marked path via Loch Gynack and over into Glen Banchor. Follow the track and path through Glen Banchor and continue to Gargask and Laggan Bridge. Follow the minor road to Garva bridge and Melgarve bothy and then the track over the Corrieyairack Pass to Culachy and Fort Augustus.

Route cont:

Follow the Caledonian Canal to Bridge of Oich and then an old railway line alongside Loch Oich to South Laggan. It's about 1.5km from here to the shop at The Well of the Seven Heads, a good re-supply point.

From the shop, backtrack along the road for a short distance to a junction with a Forest Enterprise track. Follow this track north and west through the Glengarry Forest for 15km to the footbridge over the narrows of Loch Garry. From here follow the road west, past Tomdoun Lodge Hotel to GR113018. A footpath runs over the Druim na h-Achlaise ridge and down into Glen Loyne near the head of Loch Loyne. Cross the River Loyne near to GR091055 then follow the track on the opposite shore over the east slopes of Creag a'Mhaim and down to Cluanie.

From the hotel at Cluanie, backtrack along the road for about 1.5km and take the signed path that runs over the An Caorann Mor into the head of Glen Affric. Turn south-west into the Fionngleann and follow the track past Camban bothy into Gleann Lichd. Follow the track, occasionally steeply, down to Glenlichd House and the estate track that runs north-west to the road at Morvich. Follow the road to Inchnacroe where a footpath, signposted to the Falls of Glomach, runs north then north-east to cross the river below Dorusduain. Continue on the signposted path to the bridge over the Allt an Leoid Ghaineamhaich. Cross the bridge and follow the path as it turns right and ascends the slopes above the burn to the Bealach na Sroine.

Cross the bealach and descend north-east to the Allt a'Ghlomaich above the Falls of Glomach. Follow the path down the steep-sided glen into Glen Elchaig where a footbridge crosses the river. Follow a broad track in a NE direction, past Carnach to the empty house called Iron Lodge. Just beyond, at a path junction, stay left and climb N through a pass between Faochaig and Aonach Buidhe. Cross the pass and follow the waters of the Allt na Sean-luibe to the outflow of Loch Cruoshie. Now follow the stream W to its confluence with the Uisge Dubh. Head N now to a footbridge over the latter stream and follow the track E, past Bendronaig Lodge beyond which another footpath runs north by the Black Water to Loch an Laoigh. You have to leave the path just beyond the loch and cross the Abhainn Bhearnais to the bothy on the north shore (GR 021431).

From there another footpath runs over a high (600m) pass below Sgurr na Feartaig from where it wriggles down towards the Achnashellach Forest and a forestry track that runs roughly E to the bridge over the River Carron. Cross the railway line to the A890 road just E of Gerry's Hostel. Follow the road W to Achnashellach Station. It is occasionally possible to wade across the River Carron just below Lair. While this saves about 5 miles of walking make sure it is safe to cross the river. If in any doubt, don't risk it.

The section from Bendronaig Lodge can be difficult in bad weather. A lower level alternative follows a footpath from Glen Ling north to the A890 at Attadale and then follows the road to Strathcarron. From there, continue on the A890 and a long road stretch past Coulags to Achnashellach.

A late winter's morning on the new pathway linking Kingussie and Newtonmore with Creag Dhubh in the background

Although I've lived in Newtonmore for over a quarter of a century I was happy enough to take make the short journey into Kingussie to begin the longest and toughest section of the Gore-Tex Scottish National Trail. And I started it on a brand new trail that had been created by local Kingussie folk. The Cairngorm Outdoor Access Trust is an environmental charity that promotes sustainable access to the Cairngorms area. They upgrade paths and develop new paths in, around and between communities. They repair eroded paths in the mountains so that access can be sustained without damaging the landscape and environment and they provide information about Outdoors Access through leaflets, interpretive boards and signposting.

What excites me about the work of COAT is that they are developing a *network* of footpaths, a route system that can be linked together to create longer and more adventurous routes linking the villages and communities throughout the Cairngorms. And the new route that now runs between Kingussie and Newtonmore does exactly that, a hill-going alternative to the hugely successful Sustrans cycle-track.

Andy Dunn and Dick Webster from Kingussie invited me to walk the new route with them and Ewan Thain from COAT joined us. We made our way around the top of the golf course before meeting up with the new path to Newtonmore below Creag Bheag. This is the part of the route that excites me – every Christmas I take a two-day walk from Glenmore to Newtonmore, linking together some lovely little byways into a marvellous winter walk. I usually camp for the night somewhere near Glen Feshie but the end of the route has always been something of a damp squib. While I'm more than aware of the great success of the Sustrans cycle route between Kingussie and Newtonmore among local walkers, cyclists and pram-pushers, the tarmac surface and proximity of the main road will never make it popular among long-distance walkers or backpackers. The new COAT route, following the shores of Loch Gynack and crossing the moors high above Ballachroan with the hills of the west drawing you onwards, makes a much more fulfilling and attractive route for the Gore-Tex Scottish National Trail.

The route winds up though birch woodland from the golf course in Kingussie and heads along the south shores of lovely Loch Gynack to a ruckle of stone and heather – all that's left of the old village of Auchtuchle. At first glance there seems to be little left here but when you leave the path and start looking around it doesn't take long to discern the rectangular shapes of buildings, the low walls of which are now covered in heather and grass. The village is situated on a terrace on the west slopes of Creag Bheag and comprises a group of at least 12 buildings, a kiln-barn, two enclosures, some rigs, some lazy-beds and a head-dyke. We stopped here for a few moments, for the views were glorious. Across the strath of the Spey the Cairngorms and Feshie hills stood proud, their sensuous curves and rounded shapes emphasised by the blue shadows of the corries.

In the other direction the tumble of hills above Glen Banchor, Creag Dubh and Ardverikie held all the promise of the west.

At the path junction with Newtonmore's Wildcat Trail the lads headed back towards Kingussie while I made my way through the birch woods of Craggan, rejoicing in the vast heather moors on my right that form a precursor to the high Monadhliath. The Munro of A' Chailleach looked spectacular and while it was certainly a good day for the high tops I didn't feel I had lost out. I had thoroughly enjoyed the shorter low-level walk and I can see this route, with its ruined townships, tying up nicely with visits to the Highland Folk Museum in Newtonmore. A visit to the folk museum and a wander around the black houses there will give a very good idea of what life was like in these small Badenoch villages a hundred years ago.

From Newtonmore a road runs up into Glen Banchor and ends at a parking place, the usual stopping-off point for hillwalkers heading out to bag the Monadhliath Munros of A'Chailleach and Carn Sgulain. From the road-end a footpath runs west through the glen, past a couple of unoccupied houses, and through to the old bothy below Sron na Creige at the foot of Gleann Lochain. From here a bulldozed track runs through Strath an Eilich; just before it entered woodland I left it and followed the forest edge to pick up another footpath above Balgowan. By following traces of paths on the hillside above Gaskbeg and Laggan I managed to avoid any road walking until I dropped down to the little shop in Gergask. It was time for morning coffee.

You only have to spend a few minutes in this well-stocked shop to realise that Laggan has a vibrant and very active community working to improve the social and economic wellbeing of those living in the area. The Laggan Forestry Trust, working in partnership with Forestry Enterprise, has taken over the management of the forests around Laggan and is developing initiatives linked to the forest such as an interpretation centre and guided walks, and of course part of that forest is now home to the hugely successful Wolftrax cycle trails – mountain biking with bite! The community has also been very active in a number of diverse schemes, from raising money to provide low cost housing in the area to lobbying for better television reception.

Dramatic lighting illuminates the view west from the head of Glen Banchor

On the excuse of wanting to hear about the Laggan community's plans for the future I was in fact girding my loins, mentally preparing myself for a long haul on tarmac – about 16km along the lines of the old General Wade road to Spey Dam, Garva Bridge and Melgarve. I shouldn't make a great fuss about this section of road walking – it's a very minor road and passes through some gorgeous scenery, but sustained walking on tarmac is very painful on my feet, an old condition that I've learned to put up with, almost! I find it helps if I whinge and moan a lot.

I suppose I could have cursed the name of General George Wade as I padded out of Laggan and down towards the Spey, but he's probably been cursed enough in the past, particularly by cattle drovers who complained bitterly that the paved route his soldier/navvies created damaged the hooves of their cattle – the line that Wade chose over the Corrieyairack was the line of an old drovers' road from Fort Augustus.

It's easy to imagine the Jacobites weren't too fond of General Wade either, but ironically it was the army led by Charles Edward Stuart that became the first official military users of the route. So much for building roads to help subjugate the wild highland clans! But that was the original idea. The Government had become twitchy after the 1715 Jacobite Rising and realised that the highlanders could move across difficult countryside much more easily than their soldiers could, so General Wade was ordered to build a network of roads, connecting together various forts and barracks, so that the soldiers could move around a bit more quickly when trying to keep the peace. One of those roads was the Corrieyairack.

General George Wade was an Irishman and in 1724 he was given the impressive title of Commander-in-Chief of His Majesty's Forces in Scotland. Wade was a career soldier but he has gone down in history as a road builder – in the 13 years he spent in Scotland he was responsible for the surveying and completion of a number of roads including a major link between Dalwhinnie at Drumochter, and Fort Augustus at the head of Loch Ness on the important route between Inverness and what we now know as Fort William. Wade appears to have been responsible for the original road from Dunkeld, north of Perth, to Inverness, the line of which is now mostly used by the busy A9 trunk road, and in 1731 he began work on the link road between Dalwhinnie and Fort Augustus, taking full advantage of the traditional drove road that made its way through Corrie Yairack and over a prominent shoulder of Corrieyairack Hill.

Four work parties began construction in April 1731, building the 17 switchbacks on the Garvamore side and the five original bridges, and by October the same year a celebration was held on the banks of the Allt Lagain a'Bhainne above Glen Tarff on the north side of the Pass on completion of the major part of the road.

Ruined bridge near the start of the Corrieyairack Pass – a lasting legacy to the engineering skills of General Wade

The total cost was just under £3,300. Despite that, historical accounts generally paint the Corrieyairack in various shades of grimness. Montrose's Covenanting army avoided it; Bonnie Prince Charlie's troops didn't like it; Mrs Grant of Laggan, in her 1781 *Letters from the Mountains* said it was "impassable in winter"; and the Governor of Fort Augustus, in 1798, suggested it was "wild desolation beyond anything he could describe".

North of Melgarve the track is rough and incredibly straight which says a lot for the engineer's alignments. Below the loose rock on the track you can see the cobbles of the original road and even when the surface was in its prime it must have given the carts and wagons a rough ride. One notable gentlewoman who left a record of her travels in the Highlands in the year 1798, the Honourable Mrs Sarah Murray, has suggested that the road was indeed pretty hard going: "The whole road rough, dangerous and dreadful, even for a horse. The steep and black mountains, and the roaring torrents rendered every step his horse took, frightful; and when he attained the summit of the zigzags up Corrieyaireag he thought the horse himself, man and all, would be carried away, he knew not whither; so strong was the blast, so hard the rain, and so very thick the mist. And as for the cold, it stupefied him…" Mrs Murray also tells frightful tales of travellers on the road perishing from the cold and of soldiers who often died because they over-refreshed themselves with whisky.

On the subject of whisky, I spent the night camped outside Melgarve bothy and blethered for a while with an old fellow from Dundee who told me with unconcealed glee that he virtually lived in bothies, wandering from one to another as the mood took him. "Every so often I'll go back to my wee house in Dundee", he told me,"just to make sure it's still there and see what bills have arrived for me. It's a grand wee house for the winter but when spring arrives I take to the road, and the bothies." He couldn't have been a day under 75 but looked as lean and fit a gangrel as I've met anywhere. He made me a mug of strong tea and I shared a dram with him. "I don't really drink much", he told me, "but ye cannae look a gift horse in the mooth!"

I had been hoping for a gift horse myself come morning – a spell of good clear weather would have been welcome but instead it was dour, damp and grey. As a modern walking route the Corrieyairack has been cruelly robbed of its wildness by a line of goose-stepping electricity pylons that are liable to grow even higher when the new Beauly-Denny line comes into operation. An increased demand for renewable energy means that many of the pylon lines in the highlands have to be upgraded and current plans indicate the pylons themselves will be replaced by structures that could be half as high again.

After the long crossing of the Corrieyairack Pass, Fort Augustus and the southern end of Loch Ness finally come into view

Blinkered supporters of onshore wind installations often seem to forget that new power sources will need new methods of carrying all that new power, so we are likely to see not only enormous wind farms and bulldozed roads in otherwise wild areas of Scotland but more lines of electricity pylons too. The power companies currently claim that the cost of burying the cables underground, out of sight, would be too prohibitive, but appear to have enough spare cash to bribe local communities into supporting their plans. Grim thoughts for a grim day. The noise and mess associated with hundreds of men building new giant pylons were all around me – a new motorway of a track had been built adjacent to the old Wade route, a track which provided access for the big yellow machines of destruction, the diggers, the JCBs and the trucks. Not a pleasant sight in such a historically wild setting.

After a while the track runs military fashion to the right and proceeds across the lower slopes of Geal Charn. Ahead, lying face on, is the Coire Yairack itself, with the plateau of Corrieyairack Hill just above it. Just as you think you must climb up over the corrie rim, the track turns left again and begins the series of zigzags, a terrific feat of engineering in such remote surroundings. These switchbacks allow you to climb quickly to reach the high point of the pass at 764m/2507ft. Turn around, look back and catch something of the atmosphere of the place. Away through the glen you'll see the hills of the Grampians above Glen Feshie, then the valley of the infant Spey reaching almost into Corrieyairack itself. The Corrieyairack track is still officially classified as a road, although it's currently closed to traffic because of the damage that has been done by 4x4 vehicles. It does provide easy walking though, even on the sections where the streams have burst their banks and damaged the original paving. By the time I had negotiated the zig-zags at the top of Coire Yairack the rain had stopped but the wind was still cold and blustery. I stopped by the desolate hydro buildings on the summit of the pass, got out of the wind, and had a quick bite to eat.

My route lay to the north, down the long miles of Glen Tarff towards Culachy and Fort Augustus, tucked away on the southern shores of Loch Ness, the longest of several lochs that form a long waterway through the geological faultline of Gleann Mor, or the Great Glen. Sometimes referred to as Gleann Albyn, the glen of Scotland, it forms a clear dividing line between the northern highlands and the Grampians to the south and was historically regarded as an important military area for controlling the highland clans. Garrisons were created at Fort William, Fort Augustus and Fort George just beyond Inverness, the names themselves indicating the southern loyalties.

Today the Great Glen is an important link between the town of Fort William and the booming city of Inverness and a long distance walking route, the Great Glen Way, and a canoe trail, link the two centres. A Great Glen Cycle Route had also been established but it was later decided that the experience offered was of a fairly low standard – the route was 'withdrawn' in 2006 and the Highland Cycle Forum is currently examining better options for touring bikes.

Thomas Telford was one of the principal engineers behind the Caledonian Canal. Originally planned to take 7 years to complete, it took more than double this time. Today it is mainly used by summer tourists who often queue to pass through Kytra Lock

The Great Glen Way, one of Scotland's 'official' long distance walking trails, runs for 127km/79 miles between Inverness and Fort William and makes use of footpaths, forest trails and the Caledonian Canal towpath. The canal itself was designed by Thomas Telford and was opened in 1822 having taken 21 years to construct. Some 34km of artificial cuttings connect the four lochs along the Glen to provide a superb inland waterway. At its highest point the canal reaches 35m above sea level so vessels have to negotiate a series of 28 locks, a time-consuming process which probably lends a relaxed air to the whole procedure. I've always found time passing by easily on the towpath – stopping to chat to the lock-keepers, watching the flotilla of holiday cruisers, fishing boats and commercial vessels that still use the canal, or taking time to enjoy the wildlife along the way. The Cally Canal offers a very different experience to the long-distance backpacker and adds to the diversity of the Gore-Tex Scottish National Trail.

Looking east down Glen Garry – one of the many spectacular viewpoints on the trail

But the creation of the canal was no easy task and Thomas Telford had his fair share of problems to contend with. Much of the highlands area was depressed as a result of the Highland Clearances – laws had been passed in an attempt to eradicate the highland culture; many people had no jobs, no income and no future; and a huge number were emigrating to North America or to the Scottish lowlands. It was believed the creation of a canal along the length of the Great Glen could achieve two important aims – much needed employment for local people and a safer passage for wooden sailing ships, eliminating the need for them to sail round the notoriously difficult Cape Wrath and Pentland Firth.

Unfortunately, Telford discovered a problem that had affected military leaders in the highlands for centuries. During the traditional peat-cutting season and potato harvests there were high levels of absence. The workers would simply pack up their tools and head for home – they had families to feed and keep warm. This led to Telford hiring squads of navvies from Ireland, which provoked an outcry at the time. Wasn't this project supposed to be creating jobs for local people? There are distinct and uncomfortable similarities with today. The renewable energy sector, particularly the construction of large windfarms, relies heavily on expertise from abroad. Many local jobs are promised but the reality is that a lot of those jobs go to experienced personnel from central and eastern Europe. Some things never change, although we can't blame the potato harvest these days. The canal towpath carried me along to Aberchalder from where I followed the line of a dismantled railway alongside Loch Oich, with the high peaks of the Glengarry Forest towering above the treeline and the ruins of Invergarry Castle, the ancestral seat of the Macdonells of Glengarry, a branch of the Clan Donald.

By the time I reached the busy A82 road at Laggan Bridge I was hungry and in desperate need of a coffee. I knew there was a little shop just along the road and I was also aware I needed to buy some food to see me through the next several days of wild and relatively remote country. Across the road from the shop lies the monument of the Well of the Seven Heads, commemorating a rather gruesome deed from the past. In 1663, two sons of the Chief of Clan Macdonell were murdered during a quarrel with an uncle and his six sons. The murderers' deaths were ordered in vengeance for the crime, and 60 men arrived at the house of the seven, to carry out the execution. Their heads were removed from their bodies and washed in this spring, before being taken to the Chief in Invergarry. Ever since this event, the spring has been known as *Tobar-nan-ceann,* the Well of the Heads. The Gaelic inscription, seen on the front of the obelisk, tells the story of the well, and on the top of the monument is a sculpture of the seven heads of the murderers.

From Glen Garry there is a choice of route through the massive Glen Garry Forest. Hillwalkers may choose to follow the line of the Allt Cruinneachaidh up steep slopes above North Laggan and head across the high moorland to a point east of Ben Tee where another stream, the Allt na Cailliche, runs into the forest.

A footpath follows the north bank of this stream and leads to a wide forest track, which in turn runs north-west then due west towards Greenfield and Garrygualach. From there a rough footpath continues west to the Allt Choire a'Bhalachain which I crossed before turning due north along another footpath to a broad forestry track that crosses a bridge at Poulary. The Tomdoun Hotel lies a couple of kilometres to the east. Those who prefer to stay with easy tracks can reach Greenfield by taking the forest track that leaves the A82 just south-west of the Well of the Seven Heads. Follow this track north-east and then round a big bend to the left to Easter Mandally, where you can pick up the westward track to Greenfield and Garrygualach.

The character of the land is changing now. After trundling through the greenery of the Glen Garry Forest a bridge carries you across the River Garry and a track leads up to the very quiet Tomdoun to Kinlochhourn road (the longest no through road in Britain). Behind you lies a heavily coniferised landscape, in front, bare hill slopes, completely devoid of trees. Two kilometres along the road there is a distinct bend to the left. At the apex of the bend a footpath on the right follows the banks of the Allt a'Ghobhainn and climbs to a high pass, the Mam na Seilg. It then drops down the hillside, crosses the River Loyne (this can be a difficult crossing when the river is in spate) and soon meets up with another path. Shortly afterwards there is another path junction, at the Allt Coire nan Leac, and this time a dog-leg takes you back eastwards, up the hill and through a bealach between Creag Liathtais and the slopes of Creag a'Mhaim, the most easterly Munro on the South Glen Shiel ridge. A large cairn indicates the route up to the Munro soon afterwards but I ignored it on this occasion and continued downhill to meet the track, an old drovers' road that runs south from Cluanie.

This is pretty much all that remains of the old 'Road to the Isles', and this section once ran between the Cluanie Inn and Tomdoun. This drovers' road originally forded two rivers, which were dammed and flooded in 1957 to form Lochs Cluanie and Loyne. The present A87 road was constructed around the edge. This old track to Loch Loyne is still in pretty good condition but where it crossed what is now Loch Loyne, there were once two bridges and a small wooded island.

A good track leads from Loch Loyne to the Cluanie Inn

These were submerged below the waterline and only become visible when the loch is at an unusually low level. As I dropped down from the hill, Loch Cluanie lay like quicksilver. On either side of its long and ragged shoreline huge mountains reared up, brooding in the late afternoon light. This is one of the finest areas in Scotland for hillwalking. With no fewer than 21 Munros accessible from the A87 road that runs down its length, it's no wonder that Glen Shiel is so popular. With the celebrated Five Sisters of Kintail on one side of the road (only three of them are Munros though) and the Munro-rich South Glen Shiel ridge on the other (seven Munros), the area is a definite shangri-la for list-tickers. But in recent years it has also been attracting those who move over the hills at a faster pace, particularly those whose target is to try and climb the biggest number of Munros within 24 hours. The fell-runners have been moving north.

Wild, remote country awaits north of Loch Cluanie. On the right are the Munro summits of A'Chralaig and Mullach Fraoch choire

Lochaber is historically the arena for such attempts. With the Aonachs, the Grey Corries and the Mamores providing long ridges with plenty of Munros (linking these is known as the Tranter Round after the late Philip Tranter first walked round in less than 24 hours) it's not surprising that this area attracted the record-breakers. Later extensions to this round moved out eastwards to the peaks around Loch Treig and latterly the two Munros south of Loch Ossian as well. The summer of 1987 saw what was considered to be the maximum number of ascents possible within a 24-hour period when Cumbrian Martin Stone ran round no fewer than 26 Munro summits, a remarkable achievement.

The next year saw the attempts move north to the Glen Shiel and Glen Affric area. The route started at the Cluanie Inn and traversed the South Glen Shiel ridge followed by a descent almost to sea level before a tough re-ascent to take in the Five Sisters of Kintail and the ridge of Ciste Dubh. The runners then turned their attention to the big hills north of Glen Affric before finishing across the five summits of the Cluanie Horseshoe. In July 1988, Jonathon Broxap ran the 125km/78-mile route in 23 hours 20 minutes. He climbed over 9,500m/33,000ft of ascent, 1500m/4,000 feet more than an ascent of Mount Everest from sea level, and completed a grand tally of 28 Munros. Since then, Adrian Belton has equalled this total of Munros in the Lochaber area, but it took him slightly longer. In 2008, Stephen Pyke (Spyke) set out to break the Broxap record on a planned 31 Munro route, however bad weather forced the attempt to be abandoned after 21 Munros. As far as I'm aware the old Broxap record still stands. There was a time when I might have accused such runners of missing out on some of the great benefits of the hills because they dash round at such a pace but I know a number of fell runners and I'm now well aware that their love of the mountains is as deep rooted as my own. As I get older I must confess to a feeling of envy at their fitness – it must be wonderful to know the freedom of untrammelled movement, unburdened by packs or even heavy boots, as you jog over the hills of either Lochaber or Glen Shiel. If only my knees didn't protest so much….

The Cluanie isn't only a popular base for hill-goers but also for travellers heading west towards Kintail and Skye. The Inn was established in 1787 as a staging post where the drovers and their herds of cattle turned south for Tomdoun and, eventually, the great cattle trysts at Crieff and Falkirk. It was built on the orders of Macdonell of Glengarry and it is still an important staging post. I'd booked in for what was to be a night of comfort before the next few nights wild camping. Fortunately the Inn was quiet and I spent the evening eating, drinking good beer and making notes on my onward route. There was a time when I might have disdained such spendthrift luxury, but as I've become older I've enjoyed the occasional break from wild camping, not so much from the sleeping point of view, for I usually find hotels and guest houses are overheated, but because I enjoy few things more than a couple of pints of decent beer followed by a good meal.

I left early next morning, fortified by a traditional full Scottish breakfast – bacon, eggs, mushrooms, sausage, black pudding and tomato – ready for a good stomp through An Caorann Mor to Glen Affric. Just over a kilometre east of the Cluanie Inn a signpost (to Glen Affric) marks the way and I followed the bulldozed track uphill, the views behind me over Loch Cluanie towards Creag a'Mhaim and Druim Shionnach emphasising the sculpted nature of their great corries. After about 3km the track fizzled out to become a boggy footpath and I followed this as best I could. Here and there the path became braided but I stuck to the highest path, avoiding the notorious bogs on the floor of the pass.

This particular path stays pretty high and eventually dropped down to the footbridge over the River Affric. Alltbeithe Youth Hostel lay in front of me but there was no-one about. We had stayed there the year before when we were doing a gear-testing item for BBC Scotland's Adventure Show. We were testing tents and waterproof jackets, which was useful because the weather was atrocious and while co-presenter Desiree Wilson and I braved the storm and slept in the wind-battered and rain-lashed tents, the rest of the crew took up residence in the warmth of the youth hostel. Jokingly, I suggested to the warden he give them all some hefty hostel duties to do but he doubly surprised me by informing me that he was a 'manager' not a warden, and that hostel duties were a thing of the past. Apparently they now infringe health and safety regulations!

In contrast to that day of rain and wind when we tested our waterproofs this was a day in a million. The sun shone from a blue sky and I rejoiced in the magnificence of the surroundings as I made my way across the bridge over the Allt Gleann Gniomhaidh and into the Fionngleann. Two Dutch walkers were brewing up some tea in Camban Bothy and we chatted briefly – they told me of the midge horrors they endured the night before, despite the rain. The woman still had the red bumps on her arms. The midges were still around and attacked me voraciously every time I stopped but generally it was good to soak up the wild and watery atmosphere of the Fionngleann and Glen Lichd as they tumble down between the great mountain walls of Kintail. A good track allowed me to make fast progress and I wanted to get past Morvich at the foot of the glen and up as high as possible to camp, to escape the dreaded midge. In such still conditions they could be horrific.

I was heading for the Falls of Glomach, the impressive cataract that tempts hundreds of walkers every year into this wild and remote corner of Kintail. The last time I saw the Falls was on a long walk to Cape Wrath a few summers before. An excess of rain had swelled the cataract into epic proportions and not only did the raging torrent look impressive, but you could literally feel the thunder and power of it. The ground shook below my feet and the air was cool with the icy draught of the golden brown waters. I was impressed by the sheer spectacle of power and potent energy. The downside was that even the most diminutive of streams had swollen to such a degree that every crossing became a nightmare. Some rivers were simply impassable. Indeed, as I left the awesome display of the Falls of Glomach behind I had great difficulty in getting out from below the chasm that contains the falls. Every side-stream had become a raging torrent and I eventually escaped with very wet feet and a new respect for fast-running water.

The Falls of Glomach route is well signposted from Inchnacroe in Strath Croe. A footpath links with the old Forestry Commission car park at Dorusduain before heading north through the Dorusduain Wood to the confluence of the Allt Mam an Tuirc and the Allt an Leoid Ghaineamhaich. A bridge crosses the latter stream and a good footpath begins to wind its way up the hillside before climbing gradually to the 550m Bealach na Sroine. Those uninterested in aquatic displays could always leave the path hereabouts and climb up over the Meall Dubh shoulder of A'Ghlas-bheinn, and on towards the summit of the Munro, but the Falls of Glomach, said to be the second highest falls in the country, are well worth a look, especially after wet weather when the feeder streams are swollen and the Falls are consequently a greater spectacle. The top of the waterfall lies just over a kilometre beyond the Bealach na Sroine and involves a descent of about 200 metres. As you drop down from the pass you'll notice the sprawling strath of Gleann Gaorsaic and its various streams and burns that feed the main river, watercourses that drain the slopes of big mountains like Beinn Fhada and the magnificently sculpted Sgurr nan Ceathreamhnan. All that water is harnessed into a narrow stream and then directed into a narrow, rocky cleft where it plunges for some 130 metres, twice the height of Niagara, into a deep, black chasm.

Crossing the Bealach na Sròine with Carn Tarsuinn on the opposite side of Glen Elchaig

You'll probably see the spray and hear the thunder long before you see the waterfall itself. Needless to say great care should be taken on the normally wet path that skirts the top of the falls.

I pitched my tent not far from the top of the falls, on a wide grassy sward that offered great views back up Gleann Gaorsaic. As I filled my water bottles from the river I was thankful yet again that here in Scotland we can drink safely from almost any mountain stream. Abroad, such a simple and pleasurable act as drinking fresh running water is beset with potential problems. The main consideration, and one that I'm very familiar with, is that many of the streams are infested with a tiny protozoa called Ghiardia Lamblia. Once this little bug gets into your intestines and lays some eggs you can become ill – sometimes very ill.

I've experienced Ghiardia twice; once when I spent a month trekking on the Pakistan/Afghanistan border and again when I picked up the bug from a stream somewhere in the Sierra Nevada mountains of California. On both occasions I lost my appetite, drastically lost weight, felt weak and bloated and could have happily crawled into a dark hole and died. After such an experience, when I go abroad to wander in the hills, I take a water filter or water purification tablets although occasionally it's safe enough to drink from streams that are high up in the hills, well away from man and animals. Mountain springs, for a whole host of reasons, are best of all – the spot where the water gushes, or in some cases merely seeps, out of the earth itself. This, the place of birth of our streams and rivers, is where the water is at its most pure, where it's freshest, before anything gets a chance to pollute it or taint it in any way. I've always felt such places are almost sacred.

Over the years I've probably drunk from thousands of mountain springs – I don't like to pass one without stopping and, cupping my hands, taking a deep draught of it. It's wonderful. I've also discovered that these water springs are a special place where certain types of vegetation flourish. Cresses, mosses and lichens thrive in these spots, nurtured by the pure, unpolluted water. Mosses of different earth shades too – ochreous gold and russet red, yellow and orange. Because so many of these sources tend to be high in the hills they are also places of intense beauty, and it's refreshing not only to drink the water, but just to sit beside the stream and enjoy its tinkling sound, taking time to wonder about the secret of these springs. How is it possible for so much life and vigour and beauty to be sustained in what are often open, exposed and wild surroundings?

We might refer to such springs as water sources but the real source, of course, lies in the clouds above, the clouds that bring the rain, the mist, the snows in winter that then melt, and the gentle, persistent percolation of moisture through rock and soil to emerge, bubbling, through the earth's crust. With a start you suddenly realise that the stream's story doesn't begin at its source, that tiny spring of water. Its story doesn't actually begin where it is born. The energy of its flow, the quickening of its waters, is not inherent in the spring itself. Rather, the spring, amid its austere and desolate surroundings, gives life from a source outside of itself, life of eternal duration far beyond its own tiny boundaries.

It might come as a surprise – the sudden realisation that the hidden springs, high on the hills, are an intimate, quiet, gentle expression of the eternal elements of the universe – the rain, the storms, the snow and the clouds, elements that are, conversely, often violent and life-threatening. Here, compressed into a small stream of life-giving purity, lies a tiny fragment of the titanic forces of wind and weather that encircle the planet to determine its climate. These are the elemental sources of energy derived from sun, moon, stars and all the awesome arrangements ordained during the creation of the cosmos.

The remote high ground between Bearneas bothy and Glen Carron looking south west to Attadale

It's a lot to consider, when taking a drink of water from a mountain stream…

Next morning I carefully made my way down the gorge that has been created by the eroding waters of the Allt a'Ghlomaich. The path is steep but the views back to the waterfall are sensational. Eventually the going became less precipitous and the path left the banks of the Allt a'Ghlomaich to a fine old bridge that spans the River Elchaig just west of Loch na Leitreach. From the north side of the river a Land Rover track runs west to the end of the public road in Gleann Elchaig.

The splendid view north to the hills of Wester Ross

To the east, beyond the empty shell of Iron Lodge, you'll find yourself in some of the loneliest landscape in Scotland as you tread the wild miles between the isolated Maol-bhuidhe bothy and Bendronaig and then on towards Bearnais in the Attadale Deer Forest. These are landscapes for the wilderness connoisseur and this is probably a good time to consider the route ahead of us. It's known as the Cape Wrath Trail.

For a long-distance walk that doesn't actually have a waymarked route on the ground, the Cape Wrath Trail, from Fort William to Cape Wrath, the most north-westerly point on the UK mainland, is being well promoted by a host of websites and at least three guidebooks. The websites suggest differing routes for the 320km/200-mile trail, which could be a little confusing, but at least we know that it begins in Fort William and ends at Cape Wrath. In addition, a Cape Wrath Trail Association has been formed while another site offers a 'roll of honour' for those who complete the trek. But all may yet end in unity – meetings have been held by interested parties at the offices of Scottish Natural Heritage to assess the potential for formulating one single, waymarked route.

The earliest guide to the Trail appeared back in 1996 when photographer David Paterson published his *The Cape Wrath Trail: A New 200-mile Walking Route Through the North-west Scottish Highlands*. This was followed in 1999 by a Cicerone publication, *North to the Cape: A trek from Fort William to Cape Wrath* by Denis Brook and Phil Hinchliffe. This offered a slightly different route from that of David Paterson's and took the walker out west to Knoydart before returning to Kintail. More recently a third guidebook to the route has been published, also by Cicerone. *The Cape Wrath Trail Guide*, by Iain Harper, is accompanied by yet another website, which "contains comprehensive information about the route and forums where you can post your expedition reports and connect with other walkers". The trail has not yet been endorsed by Scottish Natural Heritage, is not waymarked or signposted, but has managed to attract a massive amount of publicity. That's not bad for a route that doesn't actually exist! But it's the sort of long-distance route that most keen walkers dream of. A long tough trek through some of the most majestic, remote and stunningly beautiful landscape you could dare imagine. It could be described as the toughest long-distance backpacking route in the UK.

When I walked the Cape Wrath Trail a number of years ago the route I took was posted on a popular website – www.capewrathtrail.co.uk. Since then the Wester Ross Alliance, a community development organisation, which was set up to bring together the residents and organisations of Wester Ross to promote the sustainable development of the area, has joined forces with an unlikely source, the International Appalachian Trail. The IAT wants to extend its trail network to all countries and regions once united by the supercontinent Pangea more than 250 million years ago, when the Appalachian, Caledonian, and Atlas Mountains were formed by earth's plate tectonics. And so, notionally at least, the Cape Wrath Trail, or at least the Wester Ross Alliance version of it, has become part of the Appalachian Trail. Interestingly, the CWT is a unique addition to the IAT being a geographical area rather than a set trail – all other sections of the IAT are waymarked routes.

I've stuck with my own route, that is the route between Fort William and Cape Wrath I chose some years ago, for the Gore-Tex Scottish National Trail.

However, if you, dear reader, wish to follow a different route – say, out to Knoydart and back to Kintail via Kinlochhourn and the Bealach Coire Mhalagain, then I certainly won't grumble about it. Life's too short, dammit… Indeed, there is a strong school of thought that believes the Cape Wrath Trail should remain as a 'virtual' trail, a proper wilderness experience where walkers find their own route from origin to destination by using their navigation skills – the route will change with the seasons and is clearly weather dependent where unbridged rivers and streams have to be crossed. Other groups and individuals prefer to see a waymarked route on the ground, a single, promoted trail from Fort William to Cape Wrath. Meetings have been held between interested parties and negotiations are underway as I write. I'm afraid I can't help stifling a yawn and wishing them luck…

The route I'll be describing traces the routes of others but differs here and there because, being a passionate backpacker, I've never limited myself to choosing a route that is dependent on hotel or hostel accommodation, however much I appreciate the comforts of a good meal and pint of beer. Having said that, I was keen that in working out this route I gave myself several rough guidelines: the route should follow a south to north line as close as possible; it should allow passage through the most scenic areas; it should try to avoid tarmac and paved roads as much as possible but instead follow existing footpaths and stalkers' tracks whenever they were useful; and it should avoid crossing mountain ranges and major rivers except where necessary.

The final route is a stunner. It begins at Banavie, just outside Fort William, heads up the Great Glen to Loch Lochy and then turns north to cut across Glen Garry and Glen Shiel. It traverses the huge, empty quarter between Glen Shiel and Strathcarron, wanders past the mountains south and north of Torridon and the great wilderness between Loch Maree and Little Loch Broom. North of the Ullapool road the route traverses inland to Oykel Bridge then begins the wildest and remotest stretch of all – through the mountains of Inchnadamph and Kylesku, below the shadows of Arkle and Foinaven to Rhiconich, then to Kinlochbervie on the west coast. With a final flourish we hike over the moors to magical Sandwood Bay and the remaining clifftop walk to Cape Wrath Lighthouse, the end of the journey.

Looking south to the long ridge line of Sgurr na Feartaig beyond which lies the remote hills of West Monar

But we're getting ahead of ourselves. Back in Glen Elchaig I followed the track as far as the whitewashed cottage known as Iron Lodge then, half a kilometre beyond it, left the security of the broad track for a narrow footpath that was to carry me around the Cadha Ban nose of a hill called Faochaig and over a 460m pass into the heart of one of the wildest, remotest tracts of land in the country.

This is a landscape well described by author Iain R. Thomson in his superb book, *Isolation Shepherd*. In 1956 he brought his wife and two children to settle in a remote house at the western end of Loch Monar where he was to work as a stalker and a shepherd for four years. They were hard years, working as he did in an environment that was streaked in shades of harsh and beautiful, benign and malevolent, magnificent and often cruel. He eventually had to leave when the area, including his house, was flooded as part of a large hydro-electric scheme.

Almost at the end of the long walk through Monar, Glen Carron with Beinn Eighe in the distance

Anyone with any thoughts of backpacking through this area should read Iain's book, if only to warn them of the possible conditions they might meet, in terms of weather, river crossings or the sheer harshness of the terrain. This is not a landscape for the faint-hearted, or the inexperienced. Iain's book also gives a marvellous evocation of what life was like in such a remote part of Scotland almost 60 years ago, gathering sheep, driving cattle over high mountain passes, finding dry firewood or cutting peats, when the only access was by boat down Loch Monar. Most of the bulldozed tracks that you come across today are recent innovations.

Morning mists obscured much of the Coire a'Chadha Ruaidh Mor as I passed below but on the descent beside the tumbling waters of the Allt na Sean-luibe the sun burst through and the vast landscape before me suddenly sparkled into life. As if to emphasise the scale of things the white walls of Maol-bhuidhe bothy, some three kilometres away, looked minute, dwarfed not by hills but by an immense vacuum, a flat, waterlogged space, a bogland that gathered up the waters of dozens of mountain burns and directed them west into a meandering stream that would eventually become the River Ling and Loch Long. And that meandering course was the route I followed, five kilometres of rough, pathless walking to the confluence of the Ling and the Uisge Dubh. From there I followed the Uisge Dubh (the Black Water) north to a bridge and set up my tent nearby. The next day, all going well, I would be in Torridon. I was within a stone's throw of Bendronaig Lodge, a grand title for what is little more than a basic hut, and its little bothy. Just beyond it a rough slatted bridge took me across the stream and I followed one of the fairly recent bulldozed tracks as far as Loch an Laoigh.

Mountaineers, hillwalkers and even politicians, have questioned the whole issue of bulldozed tracks in wild and remote areas like this and many believe that all new tracks should be subject to planning regulations. At the moment they are not. There is an argument that in days gone by an estate may have employed three or four shepherds, for example, to do the job that one man does now, and to cover such a large area on foot is well nigh impossible. Argocats and four wheel drive vehicles are necessary tools for many shepherds and stalkers today. But if that is the case, and the estate have a genuine case for building an engineered track, then planning permission shouldn't be an issue for them. There is a strong feeling that many of these tracks are being crudely gouged out of the hillside to enable wealthy shooting clients who don't want to walk anywhere to travel in comparative comfort.

From the shores of Loch an Laoigh I could see the roof of Bearnais bothy, and the track that runs up the hillside beyond it. It was an easy walk across tussocky turf and over the low Abhainn Bhearnais to the bothy itself, just in time for a mid-morning brew. From there another footpath runs over a high (600m) pass below Sgurr na Feartaig from where it wriggles down towards the Achnashellach Forest and a forestry track that will take you a couple of miles east to a bridge bridge over the River Carron to the A890 road just past Craig. Many walkers will want to stop at Gerry's hostel at Craig, a well known doss amongst Scottish hill goers, but I thought I could save myself about 8km of walking by wading the River Carron just below Lair. In fact I wouldn't even call it a wade – I barely got my feet wet! The river was so low I could walk over shingle bars, jumping across the gently flowing waters in between. I'm not sure the river is often as co-operative as this but it's worth checking before the long haul eastwards to the bridge at Craig.

Achnashellach to Oykel Bridge

Distance:	3/4 days; 82km/50mls: Achnashellach to Kinlochewe: 17km/10mls; Kinlochewe to Corrie Hallie: 23km/14mls; Corrie Hallie to Oykel Bridge: 42km/25 mls.
Maps:	Ordnance Survey Landranger 1:50,000 sheets 25, 20 and 19.
Public transport:	For Start and Finish: Achnashellach is on the Inverness to Kyle of Lochalsh rail line, 08457 484950, wwwscotrail.co.uk. There are bus and services from Bonar Bridge to Ledmore and Lochinver, passing Oykel Bridge. Traveline: 0871 200 2233, www.travelinescotland.com.
Accommodation:	Gerry's Hostel, Achnashellach (01520 766232), Cromasaig Guest House, Kinlochewe (01445 760234), Oykel Bridge Hotel, Rosehall (01549 441218).
Route:	From Achnashellach railway station cross the rail line (take great care), go through a gate and follow the forest track to the top of a small rise. At the top of the rise, turn left and follow another track to a fence and signpost for Coire Lair. Go through the gate in the fence and follow the path to Coire Lair. Just beyond the lip of the corrie, turn right and follow the path that skirts the lower slopes of Beinn Liath Mhor and eventually drops down to Coulin. Turn right here, pass Torran-cuillin and follow the east edge of the forest plantation to the top of the forest. Continue following the forest edge west until you come across a cairned path running north from the forest (there is a footpath through this forest marked on the OS map but I've never found it). The path crosses open country for about 1.5km before entering another forest plantation.

My advice would be to skirt round the edges of the forest as the path through it is very sketchy and there is much fallen timber to clamber over – not much fun. Beyond the forest follow the river into Kinlochewe. Alternatively, follow the estate road past Coulin Lodge to the road by Loch Clair and follow the minor road into Kinlochewe.

From Kinlochewe follow the A832 east for a short distance and take the turn-off to Incheril. Continue through the parking place onto the estate track, turn right and follow the track to a bifurcation at the Heights of Kinlochewe. Go left here, into Gleann na Muice. Cross the river by a footbridge and about halfway up the glen (GR 070667) take another rough path to the right to climb up and over Meallan Odhar. The path only continues for another kilometre or so before disappearing but continue in a NNE direction, over the river and up through the narrow defile of Bealach Gorm (GR 093715). Descend on the north side to a footpath that runs to Loch an Nid. Follow this path north for about 5km to a bulldozed estate track which then runs north all the way to Corrie Hallie and the A832. Head north along the road and turn right at the first junction. Cross the bridge over the Dundonnell River then pass through a gate on your right. Leave the path here and climb the hillside on your left until you come across a rough path. Follow this path through the trees, go through two gates and cross a stream at the top of a waterfall. From here the path is sketchy but is marked for much of its length by cairns over moorland and past Loch an Tiompain before descending to the houses at Croftown. A road crosses the River Broom from here to the A835, Garve to Ullapool road. Head north on the road for about 800m before turning right at Inverlael. Follow the forest track to Glensquaib. From here another forestry track climbs north to the forest edge and beyond to a junction of streams at GR218873. Beyond here there is no path so make your way in an ENE direction to parallel the Allt na Lairige before descending to the River Douchary. Pick up another footpath at GR246903 and follow it past Loch an Daimh to Duag Bridge at the foot of Strath Mulzie. An estate track now runs east to Amat and Oykel Bridge.

Presiding over the Achnashellach Forest like some prehistoric watchtower, the 908m/2976ft Fuar Tholl (the cold hole) is one of the most impressive hills in the land. Its three tops are guarded by steep cliffs of Torridonian sandstone, soaring skyward from the lower pine-clad levels of Coire Lair. The track that climbs out of Achnashellach below it, and into Coire Lair, is a delight. You can cross the railway, with care, and you'll be pleased to know that Network Rail haven't seen fit to ban pedestrians from crossing the railway line here as they've tried to do at dozens of other crossings throughout the nation. The track then approaches the tumultuous River Lair where a footpath bears off to the left to follow the east bank of the river through a veritable jungle of rhododendron bushes and trees. I've never known this footpath to be anything other than running with water, but consolation comes from the sheer power of the waterfalls in the adjacent river course. What a fabulous start to a walk, with pine trees sheltering the path that climbs over sandstone slabs, crinkled and creased with streaks of quartzite that glint and sparkle in the sun.

As you surmount the lip of Coire Lair it's worth pausing just to take in the scale of things. Two Munros are the normal attention-grabbers here – Sgorr Ruadh and the long, curving ridge of Beinn Liath Mhor. The classic Coire Lair Horseshoe walk gathers both of them in, the two Munros linked by a high pass, and stronger walkers often add the Corbett of Fuar Tholl, almost as an afterthought although it's the finest mountain of the three. A large cairn, situated on a huge plinth of sandstone on the corrie lip, marks a junction of ways. To the left a path crosses lochan-splattered moors to the Bealach Mhoir, and straight ahead another path climbs the long slopes of the corrie, passing Loch Coire Lair towards the bealach between Beinn Liath Mhor and Sgorr Ruadh. A short way along this path I turned right at another junction. This new path runs in a north-easterly direction to skirt the slopes of Beinn Liath Mhor, drops down to the lovely setting of the Easain Dorcha bothy and along to the bridge that meets the track from the Coulin Pass. A few kilometres to the north lies Coulin Lodge and the path alongside Loch Clair that leads to the A896 Kinlochewe road.

North of Achnashellach Station with Fuar Tholl guarding the way ahead

The classic outline of Liathach from Loch Clair – one of the most iconic views in Scotland

I was now in Torridon and the complex geology of the region was to dominate the scenery for the next couple of days. Consider it as you gaze on Liathach, the classic view from Loch Clair, or Beinn Eighe, near Kinlochewe. This isn't so much a single mountain as a mini-chain of them, a complex range whose terraced cliffs are cut at frequent intervals by long, vertical gullies that drop down into great fan-shaped stone chutes. And if the visual impact of this hill doesn't take your breath away, its enduring quality certainly will. Beinn Eighe has been a National Nature Reserve for just over 50 years, a mere flicker of time in the life of a mountain, but at least it offers us a tangible time span to grapple with. It's rather more difficult to wrestle with the comparatively abstract notion that the sandstone of our Torridon mountains was originally laid down about a thousand million years ago on a platform of Lewisian gneiss that could well be two and a half thousand million years old!

I spent the night with Tom and Liz Forrest, who originally met each other on the *TGO Challenge*, the cross-Scotland backpacking event organised by *TGO (The Great Outdoors)* Magazine. They now run a rather fine guest house at Cromasaig near Kinlochewe and the route of the Gore-Tex Scottish National Trail passes their front door. They've been running the B&B since 1993 although the house itself is a wee bit older than that. The original building dates back to the 1600s and the present building, built in the 1920s, used stone from the original house. Beyond Kinlochewe, the only re-supply point on this section of the route, I entered a region known as the Letterewe Wilderness, between Loch Maree and Little Loch Broom. It was the poet Milton who once referred to "wilderness" as a place of abundance. American writer Gary Snyder, the poet laureate of the American ecology movement, agrees, but with the corollary that wilderness has also "implied chaos, zeros, the unknown, realms of taboo, the habitat of both the ecstatic and the demonic. In both senses it's a place of archetypal power, teaching and challenge".

The north shores of Loch Maree are rich in oak wood and associated undergrowth and the glens are full of wild flowers – orchids, bog asphodel, lousewort and milkwort. Higher up the quartzite and Torridonian sandstone ridges, crags and tops offer all the challenge Snyder could ask for and I had little doubt I would experience some of that archetypal power beyond the Heights of Kinlochewe as I trod, rather wearily, over the Bealach Gorm and down to Loch an Nid, a lonely stretch of water in a deep cleft between Creag Rainich and the great corrie bitten wall between Mullach Coire Mhic Fhearchair and Beinn a'Chlaidheimh.

This is a wonderful stretch of walking, with the long ridgeline of An Teallach presenting an unusual view of the mountain, one of the most popular in the land. The mountain dominates the Strathnasheallag Forest south of Little Loch Broom, its serrated crest reaching a high point on Bidein a' Ghlas Thuill at 1062m/3484ft.

Another of its peaks, Sgurr Fiona, 1059m/3474ft is also a Munro. But the real attraction of An Teallach is the 4km ridge around its deep Toll or 'hollow', particularly the section known as the Corrag Bhuidhe Buttresses, a sinuous edge which offers the finest ridge scramble on mainland Scotland. The first steep slab is a delight, climbing rounded sandstone 'woolpacks', piled high on top of each other for a good ten metres or so. This is followed by a level stretch of grassy scree, which leads to the crux, a steep shallow chimney, well marked by crampon scratches. An abseil sling at the top suggests the regular use of a rope, particularly

Cameron's favourite view of the great bulk of An Teallach with Glas Mheall Mor and Glas Mheall Liath prominent in the foreground

sensible in winter conditions. A tip-toe traverse along the narrow crest will have you whooping in delight before the climb up onto the overhanging spire called Lord Berkeley's Seat. Who was this Lord Berkeley? Apparently he was a gentleman who, for a bet, sat on the spire's summit block with his feet overhanging the edge. A number of years ago I climbed An Teallach during a television programme and admitted to the world that it was my favourite mountain. Perhaps I was being slightly over-enthusiastic, but I would certainly put the mountain in my top five favourite hills.

A high level path, cairned for much of its way, runs between Corrie Hallie below An Teallach and the A835 Ullapool road. I've walked up this path several times and I'm convinced it shows the very best of An Teallach. From here it's easy to understand that this fine mountain is much more than a single entity – like Beinn Eighe it's a mini-mountain range with great buttressed ridges curling protectively round two deep and impressive corries, Glas Tholl and Toll an Lochain. Somewhat surprisingly the most impressive peak is neither of the Munro tops but the quartzite capped Glas Mheall Liath, the culmination of the middle ridge. The jagged Sgurr Fiona and Bidein a'Ghlas Thuill look small in comparison. The first time I saw An Teallach from here I immediately promoted it to my number one, my favourite Scottish Munro! Indeed, at one point I decided that this view of An Teallach was probably the best view on the whole length of the Gore-Tex Scottish National Trail.

The path over this broad rump of land between Dundonnell and Strath Broom is sketchy but is marked for much of its length by waymarking cairns. It's a delightful walk with the big hills of the north-west on one side and the Torridon hills on the other. The moorland is loch splattered and I stopped to watch black-throated divers on Loch an Tiompain. Little unscheduled stops like this become so precious when walking long distance routes. The sound of skylarks filled the air and the sun felt warm. I almost nodded off to sleep and it was with some reluctance that I gave myself a shake before descending steeply to the houses at Croftown. I still had a long walk in front of me today.

A road crosses the River Broom from here to the A835, Garve to Ullapool road and a kilometre of tarmac-bashing took me to the familiar farmhouse and parking area at Inverlael. The forest track to Glensquaib was like an old friend, the precursor to many Munro-bagging days on the Beinn Dearg hills, and it felt good to be back. From the bridge and ruins at Glensquaib I left the track that runs up Gleann na Squaib and instead followed another one north-east for a short distance where an easily missed footpath on the left climbs steeply to meet a high-level forest track that comes in from the west. At that point another path, and a gate, gives access to the moorland above, where the footpath curls round a broad ridge.

The view north west to Little Loch Broom as the trail follows an indistinct path above Dundonnell

I knew from the map that the path soon ran out and it was no surprise when it did. From there it was a bit of a pathless trot over the high moorland of swaying bog cotton to meet up with the Allt na Lairige, which soon descended rather dramatically into the confines of upper Glen Douchary, or as the Ordnance Survey has it, Gleann a' Chadha Dheirg. What a feeling of remoteness there is here. I put up my tent on a grassy shelf above the river and allowed the quietude to work on me. Partly because I was pretty exhausted after a long day, I just sat in the door of the tent and did nothing for a good half-hour. Behind me rose the steep western nose of Seana Bhraigh, reckoned to be the remotest of all the Munros, and in front lay the northern slopes of another Munro, Eididh nan Clach Geala. Other than the orchestral rumbling of the river and the occasional sough of wind on the tent fabric there were no other sounds. Even the birds were silent. Unsurprisingly, it was the midges that wakened me from my reverie and got me moving. First thing was to dig into my pack for one of the most valuable bits of gear for summer backpacking in the Scottish highlands: the midge coil.

These green coils are a lifeline and I rarely venture into the hills in summer without one. We all have our own particular ways of dealing with the midge problem, and for years my own preference has been for repellents with a high Deet (N-Diethyl-meta-toluamide) factor. From time to time I've used Avon's *Skin So Soft* though I'm a bit wary of asking for it in the shops, but no matter what kind of personal repellent you use the fact is that the midges will always get you – they will always find the spot on your skin that the repellent hasn't reached. Midge coils are used differently. Light one, and place it close to the bell-end of your tent and you'll find yourself in a blessed, midge-free zone. You can sit there, at the entrance to your tent, and beyond the thin, smoky haze of the smouldering coils you can see the midges gather, a dark cloud waiting to pounce. But they can't while the coil is burning. It makes you feel rather smug and it's tempting to give them two fingers! But what's so magical about these coils? What is it the midges hate about them?

Midge coils, or mosquito coils as they are more commonly sold, are shaped into a coil, or spiral, and typically made from a kind of dried paste that contains pyrethrum powder. You light one end of the coil and it smoulders, giving off a smoke that appears to be quite toxic to midges. A typical coil can usually burn for up to about 6 hours, although I wouldn't recommend you go to sleep with one burning in the confines of a backpacking tent. I usually have one burning as I cook and eat my meal. Once I've finished and washed up I break off the smouldering end of the coil, get fully inside the tent and zip up the mozzy net. I then light the coil again in the morning before I cook breakfast. In recent years there have been a number of scare stories, usually emanating from the US, about the smoke from mosquito coils being carcinogenic. I tend to treat such stories lightly, as people have been using these coils for decades and moreover, I always burn them outside the tent, in the fresh air, and never in a closely confined space where, apart from cancer or anything else, I'd probably choke to death!

On the opposite side of the River Deuchary a broad track skirted the slopes of Creag Dhubh and Meall nam Bradhan and, after about 6-7km, met up with the path that runs the length of Strath Mulzie down to Duag Bridge and along by the River Einig to Amat and Oykel Bridge. The single-span bridge lies on the River

Oykel, 19km west of Lairg. The inn was built here in 1831 to serve travellers on the road to Assynt and is a traditional angling establishment. It's a wee bit on the 'huntin' fishin'shootin' side but hey, long-distance backpackers can't afford to be choosy!

My wife Gina and I stopped here a few years ago when we were hiking the Cape Wrath Trail. We booked in for the night and I asked the receptionist if we could have an evening meal. She looked at our soiled tee-shirts and mud-splattered trousers and, very diplomatically, suggested we might like to eat in the bar. I felt like something more substantial than a burger and asked if there was a proper restaurant? There was, so I asked what time we could eat there. Looking none too pleased, she said dinner was served at 7.30. We went off and had a bath and changed into fresh tee-shirts and trousers and wandered down to the restaurant just before 7.30. The room was empty so we just chose a table and sat down. Just as we did, a waitress rushed out from the kitchen, turned the lights down a tad lower and, taking an antique mallet from its stand, banged a huge and very loud gong! Within minutes the other residents trooped in, clad in a full array of tweed suits, collars and ties and tweed skirts for the ladies.

Everyone was dressed to the nines, other than us, and one gentleman with a florid face and droopy moustache asked us very politely if we were on holiday. When I told him we were walking between Fort William and Cape Wrath he gasped, stood up and announced the fact to the rest of the restaurant. We were given an impromptu round of applause and for the rest of the evening we were treated like a novelty act! Everyone was very pleasant, we had a wonderful meal of scallops and salt lamb and all the trimmings, and we eventually stumbled off to bed thinking that the world wasn't such a bad place at all and that anglers in particular were quite a pleasant breed of people…

Dragonfly – Wildlife abounds in Wester Ross

Oykel Bridge to Cape Wrath

Distance:	4/5 days: 104km/63mls: Oykel Bridge to Kylesku: 42km/25mls; Kylesku to Rhiconich: 30km/18mls; Rhiconich to Sandwood Bay: 20km/12mls; Sandwood Bay to Cape Wrath: 12km/7mls.
Maps:	Ordnance Survey Landranger 1:50,000 sheets 15 and 9.
Public transport:	For start and finish: There are bus services from Bonar Bridge to Ledmore and Lochinver, passing Oykel Bridge. Cape Wrath lighthouse is served by a minibus (several times a day between May and September, 01971 511287) that connects with a ferry (01971 511376) across the Kyle of Durness to the main road at Keodale, just over 3km from Durness. Durness is served by buses to Ullapool, Lairg and Inverness. Traveline: 0871 2002233, www.travelinescotland.com.
Accommodation:	Oykel Bridge Hotel, Rosehall (01549 441218). There is a hotel and a hostel (01971 502003) at Kylesku and a hotel at Rhiconich. There is a hotel and B&B accommodation at Kinlochbervie but no accommodation north of here on the trail.
Route:	Follow the well-maintained track on the north bank of the River Oykel all the way to Loch Ailsh. Beyond Benmore Lodge the character of the landscape changes and as the track leaves the forest to follow the River Oykel north to Conival and Ben More Assynt you have a choice of route. Both routes are relatively tough but the harder of the two follows a rough footpath in a north-east direction beside the Allt Sail an Ruathair and continues over the south-east slopes of Meall an Aonaich to Loch Carn nan Conbhairean. From the loch the path continues north, skirting the east slopes of Ben More Assynt. At Loch Bealach a'Mhadaidh the path stops.

Go north to Gorm Loch Mor and then north-west to pick up another path at GR304251. At GR273277 another path runs off to the right towards the Eas a'Chual Aluinn waterfall. Continue on the original path and follow it all the way to Loch na Gainmhich.

The alternative route follows the River Oykel N into the huge corrie to the S of Conival and Ben More Assynt. After the track stops follow the river as far as you can before climbing to the high bealach between Breabag Tarsuinn and Conival. Follow the Allt a' Bhealaich down into Gleann Dubh, past the Traligill caves and down to Inchnadamph. From here a good footpath runs NE then N past Loch Fleodach Coire and over the high bealach just E of Glas Bheinn. Continue on the path as it zig-zags its way down towards the Eas a' Chual Aluinn waterfall before turning W, past Loch Bealach a' Bhuirich and down to Loch na Gainmhich beside the A894 road.

You can either follow the road from here to Kylesku or alternatively descend to the shores of Loch Glencoul and follow this to the road just before Unapool.

Cross the Kylesku Bridge and follow the road to the junction with the minor road that leads to the old ferry landing at Kylestrome. Just before a gate, go left through the trees to another road but disregard this one and continue in an ENE direction on a path that crosses rough ground for 11km to the A838 at Loch More. Turn left on to the road and follow it for about 1.5km to Achfary. From here follow the track NW through the forest and into Strath Stack. Continue to a path junction and turn right, below Ben Stack, to descend to the road again. Alternatively follow the A838 road from Achfary to the bridge at Lochstack Lodge.

Cross the bridge over the river at GR269437. Follow the path past Lochstack Lodge as far as the Alltan Riabhach (GR285467). From here cross rough ground to the head of Loch a'Garbh-bhaid Mor. A very sketchy and wet path runs NW to Rhiconich following the east shores of the lochs and rivers.

From Rhiconich follow the B801 for about 6km to Kinlochbervie, then a minor road for another 4km to Blairmore. From here follow the track and very obvious path to Sandwood Bay. From the north end of Sandwood Bay follow the coastline north (few paths) to Cape Wrath and the end of the trail.

Looking north along the Trail with the River Oykel and Ben More Assynt in the background

This time round I ate in the bar, and breakfast next morning was every bit as good as the burger and chips I had enjoyed the night before, so, stuffed full of black pudding and venison sausages I followed the River Oykel all the way to its headwaters in the great corrie below Ben More Assynt and Conival, the two iconic Munros of these far northern parts. A forestry track behind the hotel wound its way through the Caplich Wood and once free of the trees took a direct line beside the river all the way to the confluence with the Allt Rugaidh Mhor on the very edge of the Salachy Forest. Once across the stream the track disintegrated into a sketchy footpath, which continued north on the east bank of the River Oykel to the little cabin marked on the map as Salachy. On a previous visit we had tried, without success, to follow fire-breaks through the forest to the north of this cabin, in search of another forest track that would take us north to Loch Ailsh, but after fighting midges and tree branches, bogs and potholes, we never found it. This time I didn't even bother. I knew that if I continued following the river, although the footpath completely vanished from time to time, I would eventually arrive at a bridge over the Oykel just south of the loch.

Just like the time before, the 4km or so to the bridge were boggy and rough, so it was with some relief that I eventually reached the broad track that accesses the ultra-modern Benmore Lodge from the A837 road. Dogs barked at me as I passed the building – it's apparently a holiday let – and followed the track north to the confluence of the young River Oykel and the Allt Sail an Ruathair. The landscape was growing wilder and more mountainous again and I was aware it was decision time. The choice of route through the Benmore Forest had been playing on my mind for a couple of days now and I had decided to wait until this point before finally choosing which way to go, a decision that would largely be based on how I was feeling at the time, and the prevailing weather conditions. The route north from Benmore Lodge is a tough and remote walk and is really only for those willing to embrace all aspects of a wilderness experience – pathless stretches, river crossings, rough terrain and solitude. It follows the Allt Sail an Ruathair and undulates round the eastern side of Ben More Assynt. In hillwalking terms it represents the dark side of the moon. After a trackless section of rough walking above Gorm Loch Mor, it meets a stalkers' path that climbs to the top of the Eas a'Chual Aluinn waterfall.

With low cloud on the hills and the ever-present threat of rain, I took the easy option – with the rugged corries of Breabag on one side and the steep crags of Sail an Ruathair and the Carn nan Conbhairean ridge of Ben More Assynt on the other I followed the nascent waters of the Oykel up through a long, wide glen where red deer scattered to the winds. On and on it went until I could see the craggy ground rise before me – the southern slopes of Conival itself. A tributary tumbled down the steep slopes and I followed it, scrambling over the rough ground, and surprisingly quickly found myself on the footpath that runs from the Dubh-Loch Mor of Ben More Assynt to the high bealach between Breabag Tarsuinn and Conival. Indeed, I recognised the spot. About 20 years ago I enjoyed a Munro and Corbett-bashing session in this area and had camped up here before trekking south over the Breabag ridge.

While Ben More Assynt and Conival perhaps lack the mountain architecture of their smaller neighbours, Stac Pollaidh, Ben More Coigach, Cul Mor, Cul Beag, Suilven and Quinag in particular, the two Munros rise from a desolate and water-scarred landscape. The rough, naked miles of their approach protects their shy and retiring nature and there is a real prehistoric rawness in their appeal. Their geology is also more complex. The gneiss bedrock rises to a greater height than on their western neighbours and on Ben More Assynt it almost reaches the summit. Add the crystalline Moine Schists that are also found here, the white quartzite blocks and the limestone glen below and you begin to understand why this area has been described an 'internationally acclaimed geological showpiece', and well worthy of its international Geopark status. The grey screes of Conival's upper tiers contrast starkly with the lush pastoral tones of Gleann Dubh below, and that's where I was heading now. The vibrant green indicates the predominance of limestone, the porous nature of which is responsible for the pot-holes and watercourses and the well-known caves of Traligill and its disappearing river. The Norsemen called it Troll's Gill – the giant's ravine!

My descent took me down beside the Allt a' Bhealaich and into Gleann Dubh where I thankfully pitched the tent near the Traligill caves. The rain that had threatened all day had turned that threat into reality. At least it would keep the midges at bay. The caves here are part of a large system that includes the better known Creag nan Uamh caves a few kilometres to the south. The geologists Benjamin Peach and John Horne first explored them in 1889, but the next excavations weren't made until 1926 when the Reindeer Cave and a Badger Cave (together with the main Bone Cave upon which Peach and Horne concentrated) were named. The caves are thought to be in the region of 150,000 years old and radiometric dating suggests that ice-free conditions with flowing ground water existed at the time. The remains of brown bear, polar bear, arctic fox, reindeer, lynx and lemming have been found here. Human remains have also been discovered, suggesting that man had populated northern Scotland very soon after the last ice sheets had melted, some 10,000 years ago.

Today Inchnadamph has little more than a hotel, a lodge that offers bed and breakfast, an excellent hostel, and a few scattered houses. It also has a long and varied history stretching back many thousands of years and was the heart of medieval Assynt. Fragments of a very old Celtic cross suggest an early Christian presence here. The ancient castle and burial vault of the MacLeods of Assynt can also be seen here and remains of flourishing pre-Clearance settlements can be found in the glen of the Traligill River. Inchnadamph is also one of Scotland's main geological centres of interest. As well as exploring caves it was here that John Horne and Ben Peach discovered the Moine Thrust, which explained why some older rocks were found on top of younger rocks, a curiosity that had puzzled geologists for decades. You don't have to spend very long in Assynt to see that the shape of the land is different from anything else in the UK. The low grey hills are of archaean gneiss, and studded with countless lochs and tarns. This is the oldest of British rocks, smoother and rounded by the centuries and scored and scarred by glaciers – its rounded bosses form the plateau of Assynt.

I was up and away early because I know I was in for a double treat today – a walk through a magnificent glacier-scarred landscape whose water drainage formed the highest waterfall in the UK, and a night in the Kylesku Hotel. For those cynics who boldly proclaim we don't have such a thing in Scotland as wilderness, let them wander past the pock-marked slopes and corries of Beinn Uidhe and Glas Bheinn to where the waters of the Eas a'Chual Aulinn, the highest waterfall in the UK, tumble down the Leitir Dhubh to Loch Beag of Loch Glencoul. They might see Scotland in a new, raw and rugged light. The stalkers' path that runs north from Inchnadamph climbs into a huge wild corrie, complete with not one but four corrie lochs and numerous tiny lochans. The grey headwall of this corrie is made up from the long ridge of Beinn Uidhe and its north-west terminus shares the high bealach with the Corbett, Glas Bheinn. That's where I was heading, a stony place with phenomenal views north and east to Arkle, Foinaven, Meall Horn, Meallan Liath Coire Mhic Dhughaill and Beinn Hee, the great hills of the north.

Low shafts of sunlight were lighting up the quartzite screes of Glas Bheinn's eastern slopes as I approached, creating a rather surreal atmosphere.

Bands of mist were already drifting in from the west and as I climbed the rocky path to the high pass between the Corbett's summit and the long ridge of Beinn Uidhe I half expected to see a Brocken Spectre, when sunlight casts your shadow onto the mist below, creating a halo effect. But it wasn't to be. Instead I became shrouded in ethereal wisps of vapour as I reached the pass and half thought I might have to get my compass out to find my way down the other side. No sooner had I started down the zig-zagging path than the mists simply drifted off, exposing a wide and exposed landscape, pock-marked and rumpled. The stalkers' path takes a devious, curving line, easing out the contours and wriggling between small, sparkling lochans before reaching a junction of paths above the Eas a' Chual Aluinn waterfall, the highest in the land. Someone has scrawled "To the Fall" on a large rock and a line of untidy cairns show the way to the top of the Leitir Dhubh, the precipice over which the waters fall. As I wandered down the path I couldn't help compare these falls with Ben Nevis. They have two things in common. Both boast the title of 'highest' – Ben Nevis is the highest mountain in the UK and the Eas a Chual Aluinn is the highest waterfall – but neither are the best examples of their type.

The Ben is certainly a wonderful mountain but I can think of several others I'd place above it in terms of grandeur and spectacle and while the Eas a'Chual Aluinn may be the tallest free falling waterfall in Britain at 225m/685 feet I can think of others that look much more dramatic. The Falls of Glomach in Kintail come immediately to mind, or the Steall Falls in upper Glen Nevis, or the Grey Mare's Tail that tumbles down from Loch Skeen in the Moffat hills. But perhaps I'm being a little unfair to Sutherland's big waterfall. I've walked up to it twice in recent years, the first time as part of a new long distance walking route – the Sutherland Trail – and with a television crew who had been filming the route for the BBC. On both occasions the waterfall had been less than spectacular, the braided cataract no more than a dribble. As a spectacle it was quite underwhelming, but perhaps I've been unlucky, and under normal conditions the Eas a' Chual Aluinn, or the "splendid waterfall of Coull" could well be pretty dramatic.

The view across Loch Ailsh to Sgonnan Mòr – one of many stunning landscapes in the final miles of the Trail

To see the falls properly you have to cautiously cross the stream just above the lip and walk a little way to some grassy terraces that offer better views of the 'tresses' of the falls themselves, but be careful. Some years ago a woman fell to her death here. I use the term 'fell' here loosely. Her husband, an insurance broker who had just doubled the value of her life policy, was tried for her murder and found 'not proven'. He committed suicide two years later. You can form your own conclusions. As you gaze down on the falls it's almost impossible to imagine that the course of the cascade is four times higher than Niagara!

From the path junction the route climbed again in a north-west direction, past the spectacular Loch Bealach a'Bhuirich and down through the bealach of the same name to Loch na Gainmhich by the A894. Just before I followed the shoreline down to the road I took a quick peek into the quartzite gorge at the north end of the loch. This waterfall, known locally as the Wailing Widow Fall, looked just as dramatic as the Eas a' Chual Aluinn and is, in its own way, just as hidden. You can either follow the tarmac from here to Kylesku – it's about 5km on a comparatively quiet road – or you can walk along a grassy verge for much of the way. Alternatively, descend to the shores of Loch Glencoul and follow them to the road just before Unapool. I chose the road simply because it was quicker and I could gaze lovingly across the moors on the other side of the road towards another of my favourite hills.

The first glimpse of Quinag can be intimidating. On dour days of scudding cloud she can look distinctly menacing, the main backbone of the mountain shy and retiring, hidden away by the perspective of the land behind steep, barrel shaped buttresses of terraced rock. In the fiery light of a winter sunset she can look fierce and distinctly threatening. But given a long summer's day, this old girl of the far north-west shows her kindly side and all the threats melt away. With a high-level start, obvious paths and wide ranging views the ridge-walks to her three Corbett summits makes one of the best high-level excursions in the north.

Shaped like an elongated Euro sign, with those steep buttresses forming the ends of the two upper prongs, the mountain's saving grace, as far as walkers are concerned, is that lower prong, which, unlike the other two, fades out into a long and gentle ridge and offers easy access to the hill's backbone. Unusually for a Corbett, Quinag boasts three summits – Sail Ghorm, 776m, the highest point on the top prong of the Euro; Sail Gharbh, 808m on the middle prong and Spidean Coinich, 764m on the southern one. Indeed, it's this southern top that is supposed to resemble the spout of a bucket, giving the hill the name Cuinneag – Gaelic for a narrow-mouthed water stoup. For years we knew the hill as Queenaig, giving it a royal and female association. Old habits die hard and I still think of the hill as a 'her'. Pronounce it *coon-yak*.

The little hotel at Kylesku had changed hands since I last stopped there but the welcoming bar, the hospitable comfort and the fabulous seafood were still the same. I was a little footsore by the time I arrived but now that I was well within striking distance of the last section of trail to the far north-west I wasn't going to let some discomfort spoil things. Besides, a good bar with excellent beer, a good range of malt whiskies and a terrific bar menu has the ability to soothe and smooth out the roughness of the day. I dumped my bag in the room, scuttled back to the bar, and took up temporary residence for the evening. The speciality of the Kylesku is fresh langoustines with dips, a bowl of chips and a glass of cold Chardonnay. What could be finer after a few days on the hill when the most succulent thing you have to chew is beef jerky? And that's one of the real joys of spending every third or fourth night in a hotel rather than camping continuously – the contrast between camp food and good cuisine seems to widen considerably, and even standard bar fare can taste as though it's been prepared by a cordon bleu chef!

Beyond Kylesku and its modern bridge I crossed a beautiful spine of land into the 38,000 hectare Reay Estate, an area I always think of as the land of the great northern diver. The bird's melancholy call seems to embody the spirit of these northern parts. The great highland writer Seton Gordon once described the wild and compelling cry as one that might come from "one of the uruisgean or gruagachan which in tradition and folk-lore people those sea-girt isles". It's an eerie sound in the half-light of a late summer evening, especially if you're camped by a remote hill-loch. This area is owned by the Duke of Westminster and it appears to be a well-run estate with an excellent track running all the way from Kylestrome, initially following the shores of Loch Glencoul before climbing beside the tumbling Maldie Burn to its outflow from the lovely Loch an Leathiad Bhuain. The track then veers away from the loch and climbs the hillside to meet another path. From here the walking is undulating with far-flung views in all directions – the finest walking conditions of all.

The walls of an old shieling reminded me of man's influence on these hills and glens as I crossed the Bealach nam Fiann and began the long descent down by the edge of the Achfary Forest to Lochmore Lodge, a 160-year-old hunting lodge that has been lying empty for some years. The landowner, Gerald Grosvenor, the 6th Duke of Westminster, wants to flatten it but faces opposition from people who claim that the building has important historic significance.

The long sloping ridge of Arkle seen in evening light

I'm not sure how strong that opposition is – Historic Scotland claim the building was visited "by a number of prominent figures" during the last century, including the present Royal Family, but is that sufficient reason to keep a sprawling and obsolete property, which boasts 15 bedrooms, seven bathrooms, a library, a television room, a dressing room, a playroom and pantry? The Duke of Westminster has explored a number of options for the building, including use as a hotel or an outdoor centre but the maintenance costs are apparently too high. Documents lodged with Highland Council state: "Having extensively explored potential uses and occupiers, there is no viable owner requirement or commercial use of the property".

I pondered on the issue as I wandered along the road through Achfary village to Lochstack Lodge. Could another chapter in the history of the highlands be about to close? We've seen the effect of the highland clearances and how a way of life that had existed in the highlands and islands for centuries was changed virtually overnight. The ruined shieling I had passed earlier high on the Bealach nam Fiann was a testament to that. We've seen the introduction of large-scale sheep farming in the highlands and islands and how that industry is now suffering because of a lack of subsidies and a fall in the price of lamb and mutton. In many areas, conservation concerns have seen the removal of the browsing sheep in an attempt to protect young trees and encourage new growth.

And now, a Victorian hunting lodge, a monument to another highland land use, can't even be given away. Although I'd seen precious few of them on the northern stretches of this walk, thank God, I'm as aware of anyone of the current windrush that is sweeping through the rural areas of Scotland and I recalled the number of wind turbines I had seen spinning merrily across the hills of the Borders. Is renewable energy the future for Scotland's highlands and islands? I'm not sure it is. It seems to me the Scottish Government is becoming increasingly keen on marine energy – wave, tidal and offshore wind, but as long as the Westminster subsidies remain as they are there will be floods of planning applications for turbines to be built on virtually every hill where the wind blows. I suspect we'll see many more wind installations on Scotland's hills before the main emphasis of renewable energy truly goes offshore.

While many hillwalkers and mountaineers can't understand the concept of shooting red deer stags as a form of sport, and I'm not sure I do, there is little doubt that in many areas of the highlands shooting estates equate with local jobs. Take away the shooting lodges and the keepers' jobs and you'll soon lose the local shops and businesses that service them. I think it's well proven now, even in these access-liberated times, that recreational hillwalking and deer stalking can live comfortably with each other and I worry, as more and more shooting estates come up for sale, just what an alternative land use would be? Whether we like it or not, very few of Scotland's private estates are run at a profit.

They are, in the most part, the playthings of wealthy individuals or corporate businesses and huge swathes of Scotland sadly depend on such benefactors, questionable as they may be to many hillgoers. But the alternatives, like mass coniferisation and renewable energy, either in the shape of wind turbines or massive hydro schemes, could be infinitely worse.

An alternative to this stretch of road walking can be had by following the track north-west through the forest from Achfary and into Strath Stack. Continue to a path junction and turn right, below Ben Stack, to descend to the road again. Unlike Lochmore Lodge, Lochstack Lodge looked to be busy with several Land Rovers and Argocats parked outside. The lodge itself is mostly used by fishing and shooting parties. A track runs east then roughly north from the lodge directly towards the steep slopes of Arkle. Some readers might remember the racehorses named after these two mountains – Arkle, and its immediate neighbour Foinaven, were owned by the Duchess of Westminster. It's amazing how many people have asked me why two Scottish mountains were named after famous racehorses!

As I walked towards Arkle it was another mountain that attracted much of my attention. Behind me rose the lovely peak of Ben Stack, a hill that is always worthy of an ascent, even if only for the view of these northern parts. At 721 metres it falls short of Corbett height but impresses as a rocky, conical and isolated peak that rises from the shores of Loch Stack in two steep bands of cliff-line. Its blunt, western nose is steep too, but beyond its roof-like summit ridge its south-eastern slopes fall away in a gentle and rounded ridge, the Leathan na Stioma. Footpaths curve their way round the west and south of the hill and the A838 hugs the shoreline of Loch Stack below its western cliffs offering alternative circular routes. It's a hill I've climbed a number of times and it's pyramidal shape can be seen from all round the north of Scotland. Sadly, the Labour politician Robin Cook died on its slopes a number of years ago. He apparently suffered a heart attack.

The trail continued towards the great cliff-bands of Arkle and suddenly took a sharp left-hand turn just after crossing the stream that connects Loch an Nighe Leathaid and Loch Airigh a'Bhaird. Excited by the openness of the landscape in front of me, I left the security of the track at the Alltan Riabhach and followed the stream to Loch a'Garbh-bhaid Mor where a very sketchy path ran round the eastern shores.

Foinaven often seems a mountain range in miniature and forms a memorable excursion for walkers who still have the energy

This loch, and its near neighbour, Loch a'Gharbh-bhaid Beag, form the headwaters of the Rhiconich River and are contained in a long, drawn-out channel with low hills on either side. This linear feature beautifully frames the blunt nose of Arkle in the distance and to the left of it, seen as a long and high ridge, lies Foinaven, the Queen of Sutherland, its western aspect broad and bulky with steeply rounded, vertiginous slopes that can often look quite Alpine in winter conditions. Halfway along Loch a' Gharbh–bhaid Beag I picked up a path, passed an old boathouse and followed the increasingly tumultuous Rhiconich River down to the A838 and the Rhiconich Hotel with its spectacular sunset views down the length of Loch Inchard.

A little way down the B801 towards Kinlochbervie lies the Old School restaurant, with rooms. Formerly the locally primary school from 1879 to 1970, Alan and Fiona Donaldson have turned it into a terrific restaurant with rooms in a couple of modern bungalows just behind the main building.

The seafood, as you'd expect in an area like this, is exceptional. When Gina and I walked the Cape Wrath Trail several years previously we stopped here for the night and were served our first course sitting outside, gazing at a truly astonishing sunset. By the time our second course arrived the midges had driven us to distraction. The food this time was just as good as I'd remembered it, but I didn't take any chances sitting outside. Well exercised and well fed, I slept like a baby...

Next morning, after a bit of tarmac-bashing on an admittedly quiet and beautiful road, I wandered past the fishing port of Kinlochbervie, through the straggling croftships of Oldshoremore and Blairmore, to arrive at a gate that marked the track to magical Sandwood Bay. I had planned to camp somewhere behind the bay but at this point, about five or six kilometres from Sandwood Bay itself, I felt curiously emotional. I first visited Sandwood Bay almost 30 years before, with my wife Gina and two young sons who wanted to hear the stories of mermaids and black-bearded sailors. In the years following that I must have returned half a dozen times, most recently with Rebecca Ridgway, the first woman to kayak round Cape Horn, in a BBC2 series called *Wilderness Walks*, and then with Gina when we hiked the Cape Wrath Trail. Without wanting to sound at all morbid, at my age there is always a tendency to wonder if this would be my last visit to Sandwood Bay? I decided that if it was, then dammit, I was going to make the best of it, and off I went down the track with a spring in my step that I hadn't felt for a while. After all there's little point in regretting growing older. It's a privilege denied to many.

I don't think it's too much of an exaggeration to say that the track to Sandwood Bay isn't the most exciting stretch of walking in the highlands. It could even be described as dull, but the end-point is well worth any amount of dullness. Here lies one of Scotland's finest beaches and the feeling of remoteness is powerful. At the south-west end of the bay a 100m high sea stack, Am Buachaille (the Herdsman), rises from its sandstone plinth. Behind the beach and sequestered from it by the sand dunes lies a freshwater loch, Sandwood Loch, and sitting on the grassy hillside above it are the ruins of Sandwood Cottage. The area is owned by the John Muir Trust.

The ruined cottage above Sandwood Bay – a highlight towards the end of the Trail

On the face of it Sandwood Bay is little different from countless other bays which dot the storm-lashed seaboard of Scotland, but there is an element of the very north-west of Scotland that I find hugely difficult to describe. I can tell you about the impressive cliff scenery and the relentless pounding of the Atlantic surf; I can tell you about the bare moorland hinterland and the bird sounds that keep you company; I can tell you about raucous gulls and cheeky seals and otters that emerge from translucent green waters to play on rocky strands; and I can tell you tales of mermaids, and ghostly sailors and shipwrecks. I can tell you all these things but never really touch on the real character of this north-west corner of Scotland. I can really only urge you to go there and discover it for yourself.

Sculptured dunes and small lagoons are a feature of Sandwood Bay

Sandwood Bay is long and wide and is backed by a range of marram-grass covered sand dunes. North and south of the bay high seacliffs face the vagaries of the Minch and the North Atlantic gales and behind it all lie miles of rolling Sutherland moorland. At the south-western end of the bay the Am Buachaille sea stack rises from the sea. This phalanx of red sandstone was first climbed in the 1960s by the late Dr Tom Patey, Ian Clough and mountain photographer John Cleare. Behind the beach and the dunes lies a freshwater loch, Sandwood Loch, a great favourite of fishermen, and sitting above it, the ruins of Sandwood Cottage, more of which later. So there it is, in many ways little different from dozens of other beaches that lie scattered around our coastline. But there is something else about Sandwood Bay, something that is almost indefinable, something that has attracted me back time and time again.

Sandwood Bay is one of those particularly atmospheric places; so much so that there are those who claim this is the principal hauling up place for mermaids in Scotland. You may smile, but a local shepherd, Sandy Gunn, was walking his dogs on the sand dunes a number of years ago when he saw the figure of a woman on a rocky strand which runs into the sea from the middle of the beach. He claims the figure was a mermaid, but might it have been a sea otter? Sandy, as I later discovered, was a bit of a story-teller…

There are also tales of hauntings, in particular that of a black-bearded sailor who reputedly walks up and down the beach wearing a cap and blue reefer jacket. Sailors at sea and fishermen claim to have seen him and believe that perhaps he had been shipwrecked here. The Scottish writer Seton Gordon tells of walking to Sandwood Bay early last century and how astonished he was at the number of wrecks that littered the beach. They were, he believed, old vessels, lost on this coast before the building of the Cape Wrath lighthouse a hundred years before. He even posed the question that there might be Viking longboats buried in the sand. It was the Vikings who had named the place after all – *sand-vatn*, or sand-water. As I dropped down the eroded footpath towards the bay and its dunes I passed the remains of an old cottage, thought at one time to have been the remotest house in the country. It's also supposed to be haunted.

A number of years ago I heard the story from the late Tom Weir. A young man from Edinburgh had been walking in the area and he spent the last night of his holiday alone in this Sandwood Cottage. As a memento of the most isolated house in the country he took a piece of wood from the staircase home with him. Shortly afterwards, curious things began to happen in his house. At odd times during the day his mother claimed to smell the odour of strong drink and tobacco and she had the distinct feeling that someone was in the room with her. On one occasion she woke in the middle of the night and could clearly discern, at the foot of her bed, the figure of a bearded man wearing a cap. More recently, the cottage has also been the scene of other curious phenomena. According to Marc Alexander in his book *Enchanted Britain*, two hillwalkers passed the night here, and awoke to find the ruins shaking and the sound of a wild horse stamping above them. Could this have been the *each uisge*, or water horse of ancient lore?

You don't really appreciate the size and spaciousness of Sandwood Bay until you have dropped down from the hill, crossed the sand dunes, and set foot on the beach itself. It is immense, and you can feel quite lonely. As I arrived a thin mist hung over the bay and at the southern end the slim sea stack of the Herdsman, Am Buachaille, just appeared as a pale monolith rising from a flat sea. The cliffs to the north appeared to evaporate in various shades of grey towards the distant Cape Wrath and there was a stillness over the place that I'd never experienced before. I sat on the rocky strand and soaked it in, feeling the loneliness and the quietude penetrate my very being. I felt wholly and utterly at peace with the world. The steady and impetuous surge and suck of the waves mesmerised me and overhead common gulls hung in the slight breeze. A small company of ringed plovers paraded on the flat rocks only a matter of feet away and in the near distance kittiwakes and fulmars crowded in on the rocks of the cliffs. On my very first visit to Sandwood Bay with my young family, all those years ago, I was aware that as I wandered back up the hill homeward bound I had left a small bit of myself behind. It seems that I rediscover that little sense of identity every time I return. This place simply grips your soul, and doesn't let it go.

When we filmed this route for the BBC I interviewed a local crofter who works a day a week as a conservation manager for the John Muir Trust. Cathel Morrison was born and bred in this area, a man with a passion for the history and wildlife of the area. I was a little reluctant to try and describe what Sandwood Bay felt for me – I didn't want him to think I was being a fanciful, and I know from experience that most crofters are hard-nosed, practical individuals who look upon such things as ghosts and supernatural occurrences with a degree of scorn. So instead of betraying my own feelings I asked him what Sandwood Bay meant to him?

Cathel stopped walking and looked into the far distance. "I've been coming here since I was a wee boy," he said. "I've lived here all my life and I've lost count of how many times I've walked into the bay, but every time I arrive there the hairs on the back of my head stand up and I have this powerful sensation that someone, or something, is watching me." Other than that curious sensation, Cathel has never seen or experienced anything remotely odd or supernatural, but he did pass on a story that he heard from a female visitor. "A lady rang me on the phone and told me she was researching her family tree. She had been to Sandwood Bay and we got into a long conversation about the place. Suddenly, she said she was going to tell me something she had told no-one else. On one of her visits, she saw, quite clearly, a family dressed in early Victorian clothing. She wasn't sure what they were doing but she thought they may have been having a picnic but one thing she was very sure of – there was a real sense of sadness about them. And then, as she watched them, their figures simply evaporated into the air."

I camped for the night on a spit of grass just beyond the short stream that outflows from Sandwood Loch. After supper I took a stroll on the beach. There was no-one else about. It wouldn't have been difficult to imagine a mermaid or a bearded sailor – but I had other things to think about, the bitter-sweet sensation of almost finishing a journey. A few more kilometres and I would be at Cape Wrath, the end of my journey, the terminal point of the Gore-Tex Scottish National Trail. Tomorrow would be a big day – not in terms of distance, but certainly in terms of achievement. I set out on the final seven miles or so under grey skies. At least it wasn't raining. When Gina and I walked the Cape Wrath Trail we had arrived at the lighthouse in a thick fog – we could barely see the white tower of the lighthouse until we were right up against it. I was hoping for better conditions this time.

I left Sandwood Bay and followed a ridge of marram-grass dunes before climbing above the low cliffs. The Strath Chailleach burn was easily forded and easy grassy slopes led me to Loch a'Gheodha Ruaidh which I passed on its west side. A short climb then a steeper descent took me into the steep-sided glen of the Keisgaig River and the biggest climb of the day – up to the pass between the knobbly Sithean na h-Iolaireich and Cnoc a'Ghiubhais. Three kilometres of moorland walking, brightened by acres of billowing bog-cotton, took me to the minor road that crosses Am Parbh, the name of the area of peninsula between the Kyle of Durness and Cape Wrath itself. The road curved round the slopes of Dunan Mor and there it was, the rather stumpy white lighthouse, designed in 1828 by Robert Stevenson.

Looking east from Cape Wrath to the lonely cliffs of Scotland's northern coastline

Beyond it lay the ocean, vast, empty and mysterious. I was at the north-west corner of Britain, the turning point of the Vikings. The next bit of land would be Iceland!

Much of the Cape Wrath area is owned by the Ministry of Defence, and large parts of the coast are occasionally used as a military bombing range. Access can sometimes be affected, although it's rare for access from the south to be curtailed. There didn't appear to be any problem today and several people wandered around, looking a bit lost, waiting for the arrival of the minibus to take them back to the little ferry that plies across the Kyle of Durness.

John and Kay Ure moved to this north-western corner of Scotland a number of years ago after having worked in the fur trade in Canada. It was in Newfoundland that they discovered a love of living in wild places, a far cry from their native Milngavie. After a few years living in Durness they had the opportunity of renting one of the lighthouse buildings on an improvement lease. They have opened what must be the UK's most remote tearoom, the Ozone Café, named after the wafts of fresh ozone that waft south from Greenland from time to time. Alan describes it as smelling like newly mown grass, pure fresh oxygen.

It was with some pride that Alan told me the Ozone Café is open 365 days a year, 24 hours a day. He would never refuse a genuine walker a cup of tea or protection from the elements. Indeed the couple are planning to build a bunkhouse, here on the most north-western tip of the British mainland. But life isn't always easy here, as you might imagine. Two years ago Kay travelled over to Durness just before Christmas to collect the turkey and some bits and pieces for their Christmas dinner. She didn't get home until the 18th January! The snow storms were so intense that the road was impassable for almost a month. Alan had to fend for himself and the couple eventually sat down to the Christmas dinner in late January. The only bonus was the turkey didn't thaw out before Kay had a chance to cook it.

After a mug of tea, some home made vegetable soup, and some sandwiches, not to mention Kay's superb home baked cake, I wandered off to have a look at the lighthouse and the precipitous cliffs that mark the most north-westerly point of the mainland, the 'turning-point' of the Vikings.

I couldn't help remembering the story of Alfred Wainwright's visit to Cape Wrath, told to me by Richard Else, who was the television producer who persuaded Wainwright to appear on television. He had asked the old fellow where he would most like to visit in Britain and Wainwright said Cape Wrath. Unfortunately it was early spring and the ferry across the Kyle of Durness wasn't running. The minibus that runs from the ferry to Cape Wrath was in the garage in Durness. But this was television – you could do anything! After many phone calls and a lot of effort the ferry was commissioned and the minibus transported over to the peninsula.

Journey's end – Cameron at Cape Wrath lighthouse

When Wainwright and his companion, television presenter Eric Robson, arrived with the camera crew at the lighthouse and the gull-packed cliffs, Eric asked Wainwright what he thought of it all. He pulled on his pipe, looked around, then muttered, "Glad I've seen it", before walking off. He was probably Britain's least talkative television personality.

I was glad I'd seen it too but I'd seen it before, several times. All I wanted now was a seat on the bus back to the ferry and as I wandered back towards the Ozone Café I recalled a rather nice link between the lighthouse here at Cape Wrath and my long walk. Robert Stevenson was the grandfather of Robert Louis Stevenson, a great writer, traveller and adventurer who once wrote: "For my part, I travel not to go anywhere, but to go. I travel for travel's sake. The great affair is to move". I suspect he might have liked the Gore-Tex Scottish National Trail, walking through his native land from end-to-end, learning of its history, its folklore and its culture; appreciating its landscapes and views; meeting its people and learning of the changing nature of land use. I let his words go with me as I picked up my pack and wandered off to catch the minibus to the Kyle of Durness, the short ferry journey and the long journey south:

"Give to me the life I love
Let the lave go by me
Give the jolly heaven above
And the byway nigh me"

POSTSCRIPT

In the course of a 470 mile walk through a country you get the opportunity to observe things at closer quarters than you would if you were to drive through it. Travelling by foot takes you into wild landscapes that most people, including policy-making politicians, are totally unfamiliar with.

How to protect these wild landscapes is the question I have pondered on most while walking north from Kirk Yetholm. I've seen massive changes in the Borders in my own lifetime, with huge conifer plantations shrouding historic hillsides, the loss of hedgerows and patchwork fields due to large-scale agro-industry practices and in more recent times the growth of industrial scale windfarms. Further north the coniferisation is no less severe and the constant drive for renewable energy sources will change the face of highland Scotland forever unless we can, somehow, mitigate the visual effects of it. But how much of a sacrifice are we willing to make? Climate change is a very real issue and Scotland is one of the few countries in the world attempting to seriously tackle the problem. Energy is another vital issue and until renewables like wave and tidal power come on-stream then politicians have to embrace whatever else is available. Giving that few Scots want nuclear power stations on their doorstep that alternative, for the moment, appears to be wind power, both onshore and offshore.

But large-scale windfarm industrialisation is the biggest threat to Scotland's wonderful landscapes, areas that attract thousands of tourists to Scotland every year. I firmly believe we need areas of wildness, places where people can find renewal, and peace! The American writer Edward Abbey once said that we "need a refuge even though we may never need to set foot in it. We need the possibility of escape as surely as we need hope; without it the life of the cities would drive all men into crime or drugs or psychoanalysis." Slightly tongue-in-cheek perhaps but I would agree with the concept. Even in Scotland, with our much-acclaimed land reform legislation and freedom-to-roam, many of us still think of land predominantly in economic terms, rather than in aesthetic or philosophical terms. How can you put a price tag on the likes of the Cairngorms, or the Torridon mountains? It's time we took the advice of another great American conservationist, Aldo Leopold. He said that when we consider land as a commodity to be bought and sold we tend to abuse it. If, on the other hand, we think of land as a community to which we also belong, then we will treat it with love and respect.

We are part and parcel of that community, whether we like it or not, but still we continue to abuse the land. We even pollute the very air that we breathe. Dramatic changes to the world's climate are obviously not enough to change our consumerist ways. If God himself appeared in some worldwide wondrous form and demanded change then we'd still think up ways of denying it. We'd still crucify him...

On the walk I often sat beside some long ruined shieling. I thought of the people who once lived and worked in these highland glens, many of whom were later evicted. Large scale sheep farming replaced people after the highland clearances and today those sheep have largely gone. Victorian sporting estates dominate the highlands and large areas of the borders and one wonders how sustainable they are in these very uncertain times. Very few of these estates are profitable and many landowners keep them on as hobbies, as playthings. While some landowners are working hard to regenerate native woodland and control deer numbers most estates are run on a monoculture basis, managing vast acres as a wet desert for a few grouse. Or encouraging large numbers of red deer, which browse every bit of new vegetation that pokes its head out of the dirt. This is surely not the way ahead for Scotland? Land reform is one answer, where communities control the land on which they live and work, and there have been some success stories like in Knoydart, Assynt and the Isle of Eigg, but large-scale community buy-outs are still a long way off, particularly under the current economic climate.

So what's the next throw of the dice for Scotland's wild places? I wish I knew. My end-to-end walk threw up lots of questions, but few answers. Renewable energy appears to be the most obvious bet and that isn't a pleasant option for those of us who treasure the wild places, unless we can find a means of balancing our energy/climate change needs with landscape conservation. I've probably enjoyed the best of Scotland's wild places in my lifetime, but I have grandchildren and I want the best for them too. I want them to enjoy Scotland's hills and glens as I have because I know the benefits of such a relationship. That's why I'll keep on campaigning and lobbying politicians to protect our wild places. The right to remain silent is no longer an option. We all have a duty to speak out for wild places, or we will lose them. But first take the bus to Kirk Yetholm, tie up your boot laces, hoist your pack on your shoulder and gaze north. Lying before you is an adventure like no other. Step out and enjoy it before things change too much. A nation awaits you...

GAELIC GLOSSARY

aber, abhair river's mouth, occasionally a confluence

abhainn river

achadh field, plain or meadow

aird height, high point

airidh shieling

aonach ridge

ath ford

ban, bhan white, bright, fair

beag small

bealach pass, col or saddle

beith birch

ben, beinn, bheinn hill

bidean peak

bodach old man

braigh brae, hill-top

breac speckled

brochan porridge

buachaille shepherd, herdsman, guardian

buidhe yellow

buiridh bellowing, roaring

cailleach old woman

camas bay

carn, cairn pile of stones

cas step

ceann head

choinnich mossy place, bog

chrois cross or crossing place

ciche pap, nipple

cill cell, church

ciste chest, coffin

clach, stony

clachan township

cnoc hillock

coille wood

coire, choire corrie

creachan rock

creag crag, cliff

croit croft

cruach, chruach hill

cuach cup, deep hollow

cul back

dail field

damh, daimh stag

darach oakwood

dearg red, pink

diollaid saddle

diridh a divide

dorus strait, gate

drochaid bridge

drum, druim ridge

dubh dark, black

dun fort, stronghold

each horse

eagach notched place

eas waterfall

eighe file, notched

eileach rock

eun bird

fada, fhada long

fearn alder

fiadh deer

fionn white, fair

frith deer forest

fuar cold

gabhar goat

gaoth, gaoith wind

garbh rough

garbhalach rough ridge

gartain enclosed field

geal white

gearanach walled ridge

gear short

gille young man, boy

glais burn

glas, ghlas grey, green

gleann glen

glomach chasm

gorm blue

innis, inch meadow, sometimes island

inver, inbhir confluence

iolair eagle

kin head

knock, cnoc hillock

kyle strait

ladhar forked, hoofed

lagan hollow

lairig pass

laoigh calf

laroch dwelling place

leac slab, stone

leathad slope

leis lee, leeward

leitir slope

liath grey

lochan small lake

maighdean, mhaighdean maiden

mairg rust coloured

mam rounded hill

maol, mull headland, bare hill

meadhoin middle

meall round hill

moin, mhoin, moine bog, moss peat

monadh heathery hill

mor, mhor big

muc, muice pig

mullach top summit

odhar dun coloured

ord conical hill

poite pot

poll pool, pit

puist post

righ king

ros, ross promontory, moor

ruigh shieling

sail heel

sean, sin old

seileach willow

sgeir reef

sgiath wing

sgurr, sgorr sharp pointed peak

sith fairy

sithean fairy hill

spidean peak

sron nose

stac steep rock, cliff, sea stack

steall waterfall

stob peak

suidhe seat

tarmachan ptarmigan

teallach forge, hearth

tigh house

tir area, region, land

tobar well

tom hill

torr small hill

tulach, tulachan hillock

uaine green

uamh cave

uig bay

uisge water

W.L. GORE & ASSOCIATES, THE MANUFACTURERS OF GORE-TEX® PRODUCT TECHNOLOGY.

IN 1969 BOB GORE DEVELOPED THE FIRST MICRO POROUS MEMBRANE MADE OF THE SYNTHETIC MATERIAL EPTFE. THE GORE-TEX® MEMBRANE HAS MORE THAN 1.4 BILLION PORES PER CM^2. EACH PORE IS 20,000 TIMES SMALLER THAN A DROP OF WATER YET 700 TIMES LARGER THAN A WATER VAPOUR MOLECULE. IN 1980 THE GORE-TEX® PRODUCT TECHNOLOGY WAS USED IN FOOTWEAR FOR THE FIRST TIME. MOISTURE CANNOT PENETRATE FROM THE OUTSIDE YET SWEAT PRODUCED BY YOUR FEET CAN EASILY ESCAPE. YOUR FEET STAY DRY AND COMFORTABLE.

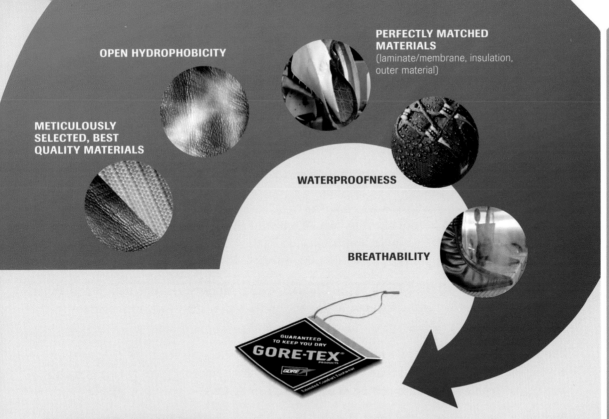

OPEN HYDROPHOBICITY

PERFECTLY MATCHED MATERIALS
(laminate/membrane, insulation, outer material)

METICULOUSLY SELECTED, BEST QUALITY MATERIALS

WATERPROOFNESS

BREATHABILITY

GUARANTEED TO KEEP YOU DRY
GORE-TEX®

CLIMATE COMFORT

As the experts in climate comfort, we have invested over 30 years of research and development in order to guarantee that our consumers are satisfied with the performance of the whole shoe. In addition to our GORE-TEX® laminate we carefully consider the construction of the shoe as a whole and the performance of the individual components such as the laces, yarns and foams. The performance of the upper materials have the greatest impact on the breathability of the whole shoe.

UPPER MATERIALS

Conventional processing is the greatest enemy that leather has if it needs to be breathable. On its way from skin to finished leather, it absorbs many different substances that close its fine pores for ever. Our partner tanneries succeed in retaining the breathability of leather by using excellent skins that only require minimum treatment, to achieve water repellency: In order to fulfill our high breathability standards our leather suppliers use finely calculated quantities of a special treatment so that it penetrates a leather without clogging up the individual leather fibres, leaving the spaces between them open. This means that the leather stays breathable.

For textiles the selection and processing is no less demanding than it is for leather. There is an enormous range of materials and only very few of them satisfy our high quality standards. We look for and choose the fabrics using the strictest of criteria. Then we process them with leading-edge technologies and test them under the toughest conditions.

Suggested Reading

Hamish's Mountain Walk, Hamish Brown. Gollancz,1977. The much loved narrative of the first non-stop round of Scotland's Munros. The original Munro-bagger's guide.

Hamish's Groat's End Walk, Hamish Brown. Gollancz. Hamish's account of his John O'Groats to Land's End hike.

Carmina Gadelica, Alexander Carmichael. Printed for the author by T. and A. Constable, 1900. Prayers, blessings and invocations collected by the Scottish folklorist Alexander Carmichael in the Western Isles in the 19th Century

On the Crofter's Trail: In Search of the Clearance Highlanders, David Craig. Jonathan Cape, 1997. The agony of the Clearances and the crofters' epic migration to Canada is the subject of this remarkable book.

Scottish Hill Names, Peter Drummond. Scottish Mountaineering Trust, 2007. A must for anyone interested in the mountain names of Scotland. A fascinating piece of research that also includes phonetic pronunciation of the Gaelic names.

Highways and Byways in the West Highlands, and **Highways and Byways in the central Highlands**, Seton Gordon. Birlinn, 1995. Revised editions of the original classics. Seton Gordon was one of the great outdoor writers of the 20th century. A walker, naturalist and piper, he straddled the worlds of the regular hillgoer and the professional naturalist.

The Wild Places, Robery Macfarlane. Granta Books, 2008. A superb treatise on wildness. Beautiful and intelligent.

Spirits of Place, Jim Perrin. Gomer Press, 1997. A powerful collection of essays, mostly on Wales, that describe the spirit of the people and the places held dear to the author, easily Britain's finest outdoor writer.

Biophilia, E.O.Wilson. Harvard University Press, 1984. An eloquent statement on the conservation ethic. Wilson claims biophilia is the essence of our humanity, a state that binds us to all living species.

St Cuthbert's Way by Ron Shaw. Mercat Press. Official guide to the marvelllous walking route that runs from Lindisfarne to Melrose

Southern Upland Way by Roger Smith. Mercat Press. Scotland's first coast-to-coast route, from Portpatrick to Cockburnspath.

From the Pennines to the Highlands, by Hamish Brown. Lochar Press. An amazingly detailed description of the route between Byrness in Northumberland and Milngavie, the start of the West Highland Way.

West Highland Way by Roger Smith and Robert Aitken. Mercat Press. The best of all the trail guides to Scotland's first, and most successful, long distance trail.

The Rob Roy Way by Jacquetta Megarry. Rucksack Readers. An interesting route betqween Drymen and Pitlochry following the footsteps of Scotland's equivalent of Robin Hood.

The Cape Wrath Trail, David Paterson. Wildcountry Press. The first Cape Wrath Trail book. More of a beautiful pictorial account of the route than a guide book but we should give David credit for being the first to come up with a route.

North to the Cape, Denis Brook and Phil Hinchliffe Cicerone. For many years the only guide to the Cape Wrath Trail. A different route to David Paterson's with a long dog leg out to Knoydart.

The Cape Wrath Trail, Iain Harper, Cicerone. The latest trail guide to a route that doesn't really exist. Yet another variation on the Cape Wrath theme but combined with a website could be really useful.

Scotland, by Chris Townsend, Cicerone Press. A detailed account of Scotland's hills. An excellent production which took a lot of time and effort.

Selkirkshire and the Borders, Walter Elliot. Deerpark Press. A history of this fabulous area, from the beginning of time to AD 1603.

Scottish Hill Tracks, Scotways. Lists of all the rights of way in Scotland. Incredinly useful little book.

The Sutherland Trail, Cameron McNeish and Richard Else. Mountain Media. 2009. A long distance walk between Lochinver and Tongue.

The Skye Trail, Cameron McNeish and Richard Else. Mountain Media. 2010. Another long walk, this time between Rubha Hunish on the Trotternish Peninsula and Broadford on the wonderful Isle of Skye.

The Wilderness World of Cameron McNeish, Cameron McNeish. The In Pinn. Essays and lots of thoughts about hills, mountain and wild places.

Minimum Impact

A number of years ago, at a BMC dinner, Jonathon Porritt said that if walkers and climbers weren't friends of the earth, then God help us all, but in all the wild areas of the UK it's not difficult to find bags of rubbish that have been left in bothies, water sources that have become contaminated by human waste, and litter crammed into the crevices of cairns and stone walls. Those responsible have been walkers and climbers.

Then there's the damage we do without even realising it. Take a typical Bank Holiday on Skiddaw. An almost continuous line of people make their way up the main path to the summit. Considering the vast numbers who climb up there the path is in surprisingly good nick but the past ten years have seen it widen appreciably and the edges have become comparatively badly eroded. Some of the steeper sections have been worn right down to the bedrock. Spur paths have appeared in places too.

The problem is numbers. These paths were never built for such a volume of traffic, so damage has become inevitable. The Lakeland hills are so popular that many of the traditional paths have become eroded scars and some wild camping spots, such as Styhead Tarn, are over-used and look worn and shabby. Yet the vast majority of folk who walk and camp in the Lake District do so because they love the place.

"Loving the hills to death" has become a little clichéd but it's true, and that deadly love affair has become a growing problem throughout our hill areas.

Much of the damage is done through ignorance. Many people simply do not know how to respect wild country. Some of the ways to minimise your impact are not that obvious and even experienced walkers can do unthinking harm. In the UK little advice is given on how to walk and camp softly in the hills, leaving little or no trace of your passing.

Paths

Hill paths are a mixture of purpose-made walkers' trails, traditional stalkers' and shepherds' paths, sheep and deer trails that have metamorphosed into footpaths and paths that have evolved because walkers have followed each other, usually up and down the quickest, most direct route. Well-located and well-constructed paths can withstand countless pairs of boots, but many paths are neither well designed nor well built and are easily damaged.

The ideal path should be wide enough for one person only, and walkers should go in single file. Walk side by side and you break down the edges of the path, widening the trail, damaging vegetation and creating more erosion and unsightly scars.

Multiple trails – braided trails – through bogs and soft ground mar too many places. Such trails are created by walkers trying to keep their feet dry. The original line of the path slowly sinks under the pressure of boots and, sometimes, mountain bike tyres, and water begins to collect in hollows, forming puddles and muddy sections.

To avoid the expanding bogs people walk round the edges, widening the path and allowing the water to spread. Over time the trail becomes a wide and muddy morass with many bypass trails curving out to the sides.

To avoid this think of the path rather than your feet and stick to the main line even if it does mean muddy boots and possibly damp socks. Where the old path is impossible to find in the deep mud try not to spread out to the sides but stay on the already damaged ground. If you really want to keep your feet dry wear gaiters or waterproof socks like SealSkinz rather than tiptoeing round the edge of boggy paths. Alternatively, splash through the first puddle and get your feet wet. After that it doesn't matter.

Zigzags or switchbacks are often found on traditional stalkers' paths and paths that have been realigned. Such paths are easier to climb and less likely to erode than paths that take a direct line up the hill. A zigzagging path can be a joy to climb and is much easier on the knees in descent than a steep one. However, too often people choose a direct line and cut the corners of zigzags. This damages the vegetation, which results in the soil breaking down and ruts appearing. This creates a watercourse for rain water and soon becomes a flowing stream.

The destructive qualities of running water are immense, so what begins as an innocent shortcut soon becomes an eroded scar. On some paths it can be hard to follow the original line so many shortcuts have been made. As well as ignoring shortcuts you can block them off with rocks or stones to discourage others from using them so the land has a chance to heal itself.

Path maintenance and construction work is grossly expensive and many agencies simply can't afford it. In Scotland alone it's been estimated that bringing all the popular mountain footpaths into good order would cost upwards of £50M. Where path repairs are being carried out it's only sensible to follow the requests of the work party to prevent further damage being done. And when repairs have been completed stick with the new path so that damaged areas can recover.

New paths can certainly stand out like a sore thumb and may initially look worse than the scars they replace but in time they weather and blend into the hillside, allowing the damaged areas to heal.

Off Trail

Going off-trail can be both exciting and adventurous and offers a closer connection with the land. Off-trail travel allows you to go where you want, not where the path takes you, but on the other hand the potential for damage is great. The main thing to avoid is creating a new path. Building waymarking cairns for others to follow is both irresponsible and environmentally damaging. A group should spread out too and not walk in single file, as this could create the beginnings of a path that could steadily evolve into erosion as others follow.

Uncontrolled dogs can cause untold problems. As they range wide they can create havoc amongst ground nesting birds while their owners walk blissfully onwards, completely unaware of the death and destruction being caused by their pet. Dogs should always be kept on a lead or kept under close control. If you have the slightest doubt about their behaviour, leave them at home.

Wild Camping

Regularly used pitches in the hills are all too often very obvious due to the rings of stones on the ground, patches of bare dirt or flattened vegetation and litter sticking out from under rocks. Often there is a network of paths too, leading to the nearest water, back to the main path and off into areas used for toilets.

When using a site like this try not to spread the damage any further and, if possible, try to reduce it. It might seem a good idea not to use such sites but what's the sense in spreading the damage into pristine areas? If possible regularly used sites should be tidied up and any litter removed.

Rings of stones, often used to hold down tent pegs, can be broken up and the stones returned to the nearest pile of rocks or the holes in the ground where they came from. Rings of stones pockmark vegetation and destroy the wild feel of a place and over the years the authors have spent hours dismantling such rings, not to mention waymarking cairns and rock windbreaks.

Often backpackers will pitch their tent on pristine ground. Your intention should be to leave no sign of your camp. First and foremost this means camping on durable ground that won't be easily damaged. Dry ground or at least well-drained ground is best for this as soft ground is easily marked. Such sites are more comfortable too. If your site does start to flood move your tent rather than dig drainage ditches.

A good site is found not made. If you need to clear vegetation or rocks to turn somewhere into a campsite it's better to go elsewhere.

When walking round a site or going to fetch water stick to hard ground if possible and try not to create the beginnings of a use-trail. If you carry a large water container you can collect all you need in one go so you don't have to tramp back and forth to the nearest stream or pool, possibly damaging the bank and making a path that others may follow.

Unless there's no choice don't camp close to water however, camp at least 50 metres from water sources, especially small upland lakes, as you may disturb animals and birds that live there and depend on this habitat. Wild sites should ideally only be used for one night. If you want to stay in the area longer move your camp unless it's on a really durable surface such as bare ground. Staying in the same place for several nights can damage the vegetation under your tent, leaving a scar and a string of little paths round the site.

Before leaving a pitch check nothing has been left behind, including any scraps of litter or crumbs of food, and fluff up any flattened vegetation. It should look as pristine as when you arrived.

Cooking

Campfires are traditional, romantic and potentially very damaging. In dry conditions there is always a fire risk, especially in peaty areas or in woodland, and what dead wood there is should be left for the animals, birds and insects that live in it.

Unless carefully built and sited fires leave scars too, blackening rocks and leaving bald patches of burnt earth. The only place a fire can be environmentally acceptable is on the seashore if there is plenty of washed up wood. Use a stove for cooking and if you're cold don't build a fire, put on more clothes or get into your sleeping bag.

Low profile stoves have been known to scorch vegetation so it's best to find a flat rock to stand them on. If the midges and the rain allow you to cook outside your tent porch look for an environmentally sensitive kitchen site. Bare ground or rock is ideal. Soft vegetation is easily damaged.

Alterations to kitchen areas should be unnecessary. If you want a seat sit on a rock or your sleeping pad. Try to keep the kitchen area clean as spilt food can attract scavenging birds like crows and gulls that may then prey on local species. If you do drop or spill anything it's best to pick it up straight away. It's easy to forget otherwise.

(This applies to lunch and snack stops too. There is evidence, for example, that the crow and gull population in some parts of the Cairngorms has increased in part because of food scraps left by walkers.)

Food scraps includes food that has burnt onto your pan. Scrape this off and into a plastic bag and take it home for disposal. Wash dishes and pans away from water too and dump the wastewater into vegetation. Never bury food scraps in the ground. Hungry animals will simply dig it up and leave a hole.

Sanitation

We are fortunate that we still have clean water in our hills. If we want it to stay this way then sensible toilet practices are essential. What this means is burying faeces and toilet paper or, preferably, carrying it out in a sealed plastic bag. (Loo paper can be burnt but only if there's absolutely no chance of starting a fire.)

Toilet sites should be situated at least 30 metres from running water if possible (difficult in some wet areas). They should also be well away from paths and anywhere people might camp or stop for lunch. Carry a small trowel to dig a hole. In winter an ice axe can be used – though there's no point is just burying excrement in snow. Sooner or later the snow will melt and the shit will still be there. Instead, find some bare ground or somewhere where the snow cover is thin.

The American *Leave No Trace* programme is a highly successful project to promote responsible outdoor recreation. It uses a simple set of principles which help minimize our impact on the environment we value and enjoy. These principles include:

1 Plan ahead and prepare

- Know the regulations and special concerns for the area you'll visit.
- Prepare for extreme weather, hazards, and emergencies.
- Schedule your trip to avoid times of high use.
- Visit in small groups. Split larger parties into groups of four to six people.

2 Travel and camp on durable surfaces

In popular areas:

- Use existing paths and campsites.
- Walk in single file in the middle of the path even when wet and muddy.
- Keep campsites small. Focus activity in areas where vegetation is absent.

In pristine areas:

- Disperse use to prevent the creation of campsites and paths.
- Avoid places where impacts are just beginning.
- Protect water sources by camping at least 50 metres from lochs and burns.
- Good campsites are found, not made. Altering a site is not necessary.

3 Dispose of waste properly

- Pack it in, pack it out. Inspect your campsite and rest areas for trash or spilled foods. Pack out all trash, leftover food, and litter.
- Deposit solid human waste in catholes dug at least fifteen to twenty centimeters deep at least 50 metres from water, camp, and trails. Cover and disguise the cathole when finished.
- Pack out toilet paper and hygiene products.
- To wash yourself or your dishes, carry water 50 metres away from streams or lochs and use small amounts of biodegradable soap. Scatter strained dishwater.

4 Leave what you find

- Preserve the past: examine, but do not touch, cultural or historic structures and artifacts.
- Leave rocks, plants and other natural objects as you find them.
- Avoid introducing or transporting non-native species.
- Do not build structures, furniture, or dig trenches.

5 Minimise campfire impacts

- Campfires can cause lasting impacts to the backcountry. Use a lightweight stove for cooking and enjoy a candle lantern for light.
- Where fires are permitted, use established fire rings, fire pans, or mound fires.
- Keep fires small.
- Only use sticks from the ground that can be broken by hand.
- Burn all wood and coals to ash, put out campfires completely, then scatter cool ashes.

6 Respect wildlife

- Observe wildlife from a distance. Do not follow or approach them.
- Never feed animals.
- Protect wildlife and your food by storing rations and trash securely.
- Control pets at all times, or leave them at home.
- Avoid wildlife during sensitive times: mating, nesting, raising young, or winter.

7 Be considerate of other visitors

- Respect othger visitors and protect the quality of their experience.
- Be courteous,. Yield to other users on the trail.
- Let nature's sounds prevail. Avoid loud voices and noises.

You can learn more at the *Leave No Trace* website at www.LNT.org.

OS MAPS   1:50,000

1 Km squares

1 Km = 2cm or 20mm

1 Mile = 1¼" (approx) + ¹⁄₃₂"

5 Miles = 6 ⁵⁄₁₆"

10 Miles = 12 ⁵⁄₈"

15 Miles = 18 ¹⁵⁄₁₆" (19")

Km to Miles   × 0.62137119224 (1·6214)

Miles to Km   × 1·609344 (1·61)